FATHERS OF THE DESERT

Marcel Driot

Fathers of the Desert

Life and spirituality

 St Paul Publications

Original title: *Les Pères du Desert. Vie et Spiritualité.*
© 1991 Editions Médiaspaul, Paris

Translated by Florestine Audette RJM

Cover: Icon of St Onuphre and St Tekla Haymanot the Ethiopian (St Mercurius Church, Old Cairo). Photo by Monica Rene.

St Paul Publications
Middlegreen, Slough SL3 6BT, United Kingdom

© St Paul Publications UK 1992
ISBN 085439 398 6
Printed by The Guernsey Press Co. Ltd, Guernsey C.I.

St Paul Publications is an activity of the priests and brothers of the Society of St Paul who proclaim the Gospel through the media of social communication

Contents

The author wishes to thank
the Bellefontaine and the Solesmes publishers
for permission to reproduce texts which are their copyright.

Introduction

This book grew out of the awareness of a certain ignorance. Some years ago I was asked to give a series of talks
at a retreat. The retreat, which was organized in the monastery I belong to, was open to members of the public. I
decided to talk about the Fathers of the Desert, a theme
which was in harmony with my lifestyle of a monk and
hermit.

It was then that a general lack of appreciation for the
subject among my listeners became obvious to me. "The
Fathers of the Desert? Never heard of them," a retreatant
told me. A priest asked me for some references of works
on the subject. "In the seminary," he said, "there was a
short course on the subject, but that was a long time ago!"

These conferences were subsequently printed in *Ecoute*,
a periodical on spirituality, published by my monastery of
La Pierre-qui-Vire. Following their publication, a bishop
called from Jerusalem requesting the complete series to
be dispatched to him. A pastor suggested that I should
give conferences on the subject in Switzerland during the
Week for Unity. The talks were also translated and published in a Spanish periodical.

A book about these monks of ancient times would
make them known to a wider public. They have left us a
legacy of writings, full of sound common sense and spiritual wisdom.

*

"The Fathers of the Desert." The expression evokes a forbidding austerity. At the time of the retreat I have just mentioned, someone had admitted his misgivings: "This series of conferences is going to be rather boring." But he soon discovered that his fears were unfounded. In fact, the Fathers of the Desert are not boring people. And if this work has the effect of a soporific, the blame must be laid on the author and not on the Fathers of the Desert.

*

As for those inhabitants of the desert, I often let them speak for themselves. Whatever I have added is not scholarly, for this book, which is not addressed to experts, is meant to be "practical". To make the Fathers of the Desert better known to the ordinary readers has been my main concern. The most important message from the Fathers of the Desert is the constant search for God. May we have the wisdom to accept it.

Please Note: The quotations are borrowed from works you will find listed in the bibliography at the end of the book. Most of these texts are called *apophthegms*. This term recurs often; there is no other better known word which is its exact synonym. The apophthegms are the "sayings of the elders": maxims, spiritual counsels, edifying stories. In the desert, they were used in the formation of the young, and of the not so young. I have also used at random terms such as: Father, Abba, Elder, Old Man. They are practically synonymous and designate those who have acquired an outstanding spiritual maturity. When we speak of an "old man" in the ancient monastic literature, we must not necessarily think of a monk advanced in years. The word always designated a man filled with the Spirit and who could also be relatively young.

1

Christians to be rediscovered

"In the mountains there were, as it were, tents filled with divine choruses of men chanting psalms, studying, fasting, praying, exulting in the hope of the good things to come and labouring in order to give alms. Mutual love and harmony reigned among them."

"We find men who had fled from the city and taken refuge in the desert even if, by nature, man is a social and civilized animal. But the perverted demons to whom they had surrendered themselves would urge them on to this misanthropy."

These two texts, quoted from contemporary writers and so markedly in contrast with each other, are both about the Fathers of the Desert. Here is what an author – this time, a modern one – has written about Anthony the Great, who bears the glorious name of "Father of the monks", and about the vast influence he had, thanks to his *Life* written by St Athanasius: "No period in the moral history of humanity possibly stirs up an interest as deep and disquieting as this asceticism of epidemic proportions. A hideous, demented, disfigured and emaciated man, bereft of knowledge, patriotism, natural affection, and dedicated to the prolonged routine of useless and atrocious tortures he inflicted upon himself and trembling in the presence of the terrifying ghosts born from his delirious mind, had become the ideal of nations who had known the works of Plato and Cicero and the lives of Socrates and Cato."[1]

These contrasting judgements made on the Fathers of the Desert show how they are not always readily understood.

Today, while being kindly disposed and understanding toward them, we may, nevertheless, legitimately ask ourselves whether the story of the Fathers of the Desert can be for us anything other than ancient history.

It is true that we find in them expressions and behaviour patterns necessarily linked to the culture and mentality of the period. However, a reading of the abundant literature they have left us shows that there also exists a positive element which clearly outweighs the negative one. We can say that the story of the Fathers of the Desert becomes a part of the Church's legacy like a treasure upon which the whole people of God must be able to draw. In the same way we can say that, for example, the Benedictine spirituality, or the works of a St John of the Cross or of a St Teresa of Avila do not belong exclusively to particular religious families but to everybody.

The Fathers of the Desert, above all, were *Christians*, trying, as we all do, to live the Gospel as fully as possible. Even if they resorted to special means to achieve their aim, they are worth rediscovering and may have a very timely message for us. This is what I would like to bring out in the following pages.

*

But, precisely, who were these men and women – for there were women among them, a fact we are apt to forget – whom we call Fathers (and Mothers) of the Desert? Let us take a brief look at their history.

The Fathers of the Desert were the first Christian monks. The origin of the movement is quite complex. It is a fact that persecutions drove the Christians out into the desert. But, paradoxically, the era of religious peace that followed led others to seek a kind of substitute for martyrdom, then considered to be the necessary way to holiness, to seek a life of solitude, self-abnegation, penance. (In the early Church, only those who had shed their blood for the faith were recognized as saints, St Martin being the first non-martyr to be canonized.) People would speak of a *white* martyrdom in connection with the Fathers of the Desert, as opposed to a *red* martyrdom, the martyrdom of the blood.

In a text of the times we read: "The man who voluntarily inflicts suffering upon himself is ranked among the martyrs by God, for his tears are valued as drops of blood."[2]

A tradition also establishes a link between the origin of monastic life and the apostolic community in Jerusalem, such as it is portrayed in the *Acts of the Apostles*.[3] In reaction to a Church inclined to become settled and lukewarm, people sought to revive a more generous, purer, more evangelical Christianity away from cities.

To these explanations we should add others, some possibly not so noble, for "flaws" are necessarily part of a movement of this scope. And so, some historians think of possible cases where economic motives drove people from the cities into the desert (they had had enough of paying taxes). Perhaps this or that one was fleeing from the state police! But these dubious vocations made up a very small minority. This phenomenon, let us point out in passing, is quite usual.[4]

Whatever the explanations about the origin of monastic life may be, as early as the third century, the deserts became peopled with those seeking this particular style of life, also called the *ascetic life*. First in Egypt, then in

Syria and Palestine, the movement struck root. Some look to Anthony, famous for his temptations and his struggles against the devil, and led a solitary or semi-solitary life. Others became disciples or spiritual sons of St Pachomius, living in very numerous and well-structured communities.

These comments of a historical order do not fully explain the phenomenon. A spiritual motivation must be added to this.

The desert Father was a *monk*. This word has taken on diverse meanings in the course of centuries. Originally, scholars tell us, it meant the consecrated celibate. Essentially, the monk seeks to become a unified being by living for God alone. However, the love of God does not exclude the love of neighbour. For the monk, as for any Christian, the two precepts of charity are inseparable, even if his withdrawal from the world alters the nature of his love. According to a famous expression borrowed from ancient monasticism, "the monk is one who separates himself from everybody in order to be united to everyone."

The monk goes *to the desert*. The place where he withdraws is part of his vocation. Nourished by Scripture, he knows that the desert is an important biblical theme bearing a twofold meaning.

The desert is the dwelling place of demons. That has already been said in the Gospel: Jesus is led to this barren and inhospitable place to be tempted by the devil (Mt 4:1). "Go away from our place! What are you doing here?" the demon cried out to Anthony.[5] Like Christ, the desert Father will fight this enemy of humankind.

If the devil is a formidable adversary for the monk, the opposite is also true. The following story testifies to this. One day Satan held a meeting in a pagan temple. One of the leaders of his army came and bowed down before him saying: "I was in such a region and I provoked people into fights; I caused a great deal of bloodshed and I have come here to tell you." Satan asked him, "How long did it take you to do that?" "Thirty days." Then he ordered him to be beaten, saying: "Is that all you did in all that time?"

Another came up and bowed down and said, "I was on the sea and I raised a storm. Boats sank and there were many victims." "How long did it take you to do that?" "Twenty days." He also was punished. Again another declared in his turn, "I was in the desert. For forty years I fought with a monk, and tonight I managed to make him fall into sin." At those words, Satan stood up, embraced him and placed his own crown on his head and made him sit on his throne: "So you were able to perform this great deed!"[6]

In another account, the author shows us Anthony walking in the desert in search of the grotto, the place where Paul of Thebes, the first hermit, lived. Anthony meets legendary creatures who show him the way. One of them is a satyr. This strange creature even offers him dates and strikes up a conversation. To Anthony's questions he replies, "I am one of the inhabitants of the deserts; the pagans, who let themselves be carried away in so many different errors, worship us under the names of fauns, satyrs and incubi." Then he asked for prayers and fled.[7]

By this account full of imagery, the author seems to want to tell us that the desert, the domain of evil spirits (even the fauns were possibly devils according to an author of the times) is "christianized" by the presence of the monks. While they admit they are bound to Satan, these miserable creatures reach the point of submitting to Jesus Christ and put themselves in the service of the friends of God.

In Scripture, the desert is also the place for a privileged encounter with God. That is where, in the past, the Lord had led his people in order to purify them. The "people" is each person taken individually. The monk in the desert

13

knows that, and he will relive the spirituality of the Exodus.

The Fathers of the Desert have not revealed to us much about their intimate life with God. Who would be surprised at that? Besides, if they had wanted to, could they have done so? That is a reserved area in their lives, an incommunicable secret.

*

Those first monks came from far and near and from every walk of life. They mention a hermit, still a slave, who every year faithfully handed over his wages to his masters in spite of the latter's reluctance in accepting this sum from one whom they revered and called "Abba". Another had been a shepherd. A great one among the great, Arsenius, a cultured Roman, had been the tutor of emperor Theodosius' children.

These extreme differences in social origins also occurred among women. A Roman lady of high rank, Paula, her daughter Eustochium and other companions of more modest conditions, rivalled with the men in the practice of all the monastic virtues. Melania the Younger (to distinguish her from her grandmother) had freed her many slaves and some among these decided to live the monastic life with her. She had become their sister and even their servant.

The moral life of their early years also distinguished these men who, nevertheless, were called to the same vocation. Anthony is presented to us by his biographer as a young man, the personification of purity itself, belonging to a good Christian family, while another desert Father, Moses, also famous, had been a brigand.

As happens at all times, God was making use of events and circumstances to "beckon" those whom he wanted for this kind of life.

Ammon the Nitriot had married against his will at the age of twenty-two. But he and his companion, without even consummating their marriage, lived a monastic life, together at first, then separately.

Paul, nicknamed the Simple, became the disciple of Abba Anthony after leaving his wife whom he had caught red-handed in the act of adultery. An ambiguous vocation. But Anthony put him through severe tests and then acknowledged he had received an authentic call from God.

A soldier, in the course of a battle, vowed that he would become a monk if he escaped the spear of the enemy. He was saved and he fulfilled his vow.

Naturally, God was using the virtues of some to convert others and bring them to monastic life.

A young brother met a priest, a worshipper of idols, and challenged him in this way: "Ah, Ah! Damon, where are you running to?" The other, furious, beat him with a stick, left him half dead and went on his way. A little further on, he met an old monk who greeted him and spoke to him kindly. Astonished, he asked, "What good do you see in me that you greet me thus?" The old monk replied, "It is because I saw you wearying yourself without realizing that this was all in vain." The idolater answered, "As for me, I was touched by your greeting and thus I learned that you come from God." After that the worshipper of idols joined the monastic life. Moreover, he persuaded others to do the same.[8]

We also find what could be called family vocations. Ammonios, his three brothers and two sisters led an ascetic life in the desert at some distance from each other. Anoub and his six brothers lived together in an old pagan temple. We are also told that several abbas had come to the desert with their sons.

They knew how to be flexible in their way of life and each one's possibilities were taken into account. A certain

15

Apollonios, a former merchant, joined a community. Since his advanced age prevented him from learning one of the trades practised in these places, he busied himself in this way: he bought supplies and medication on his trips to Alexandria and then went around to the monasteries bringing things useful to the sick. Thus, we are told, "he had found a style of life suited to his old age."[9]

*

In ancient monastic literature we find a rather important proportion of wonders: miracles, visions, revelations. Not all of these should be taken literally. The elders easily mixed stories with history. For them, the ideal was not, as it is in our modern culture, to relate facts as objectively as possible but to edify. Nevertheless, this element of wonder, as I shall have occasion to show, illustrates a most profound perception of faith. We should not conclude that nothing of supernatural nature ever occurred among the Fathers of the Desert. We must be neither too credulous nor too rationalistic. What is certain is that today, in most cases, it is practically impossible to sort out what could effectively have taken place from what belongs to a literary genre. Whether the facts are real or not matters little basically. What is important for us is to observe how these men and women lived. A story always reflects the mentality of a person and his or her milieu: it is never totally unfounded.

Two versions of what appears to be the same apophthegm shows us an interesting development moving toward the miraculous for the purpose of edification:

An abba, in order to test the spirit of obedience of his young disciple, asked him to plant a piece of dead wood and to water it every day. "Perhaps it will grow again," he said. Obviously, the wood did not come back to life and after some time the old man told the brother to discontinue.

We know enough about the methods of formation used in the desert to believe that this story is authentic. In the second version, we are told that God miraculously made this wood come back to life in order to commend the young brother's obedience.[10]

Numerous apophthegms, however, show us that the monks in the desert were not too fond of miracles. They even mistrusted them and put people on their guard against them.

We are told that one elder was granted a charism after praying God for seven years to obtain it. Another one, upon learning this, said to him with sadness: "Good work! This gift will be of no benefit to you. Now ask God to take it away from you." This he did and the charism was taken away from him.[11]

A hermit had persevered for thirty years. One day he said to himself, "I have now spent so many years here and I have had no vision and performed no miracle as did the Fathers who were monks before me." And he was tempted to go back into the world. Then he was told, "What miracle do you want to perform that would be more extraordinary than the patience and courage God has given you and which allowed you to persevere for so long?"[12]

Someone asked an old man, "How can some say that they have visions of angels?" He replied, "Happy the one who constantly sees his shortcomings before him!"[13]

The Fathers of the Desert knew that salvation does not depend on exceptional or spectacular deeds which this or that charism would allow them to perform. Someone asked an abba, "What must we do to be saved?" He was busy at his humble task of wickerwork. Without even raising his eyes, he replied, "As you see."[14]

They also knew that the devil can easily deceive those who love the miraculous. A few brothers came to see Abba Anthony to tell him about the visions they had and to find out from him if they were from God. It so happened that their donkey had died along the way. The old man, anticipating what they were to tell him, asked, "How did the little donkey die on the way?" Surprised, they asked him, "Who told you that, Abba?" "The devils did." He then taught them how they should mistrust visions and revelations.[15]

Mistrust and prudence in this domain do not imply pure and simple rejection but discernment, which is not always easy to make.

*

Moses, the former brigand mentioned earlier, was not the only one to have wielded the sword among the inhabitants of these places, who led a life sometimes described as "angelic". The story of another converted bandit, David, who eventually entered religious life, is worth telling. This will enable us to bring out a particularly appealing aspect of the story of the Fathers of the Desert.

Touched by grace, this David knocked at the door of a monastery and asked to be admitted. The abba, knowing who he was, refused to admit him. The refusal was not on account of his past activities as a brigand, but for other very plausible reasons. "You are already rather advanced in years," he objected, "you will never be able to comply with our observances; that will be too difficult for you." The other insisted, but the abba persisted in his refusal. Then the brigand told him in no uncertain terms, "If you refuse to accept me, I will fetch my band and we will put you all to the sword and destroy the monastery." Fearing the worst, the abba yielded and admitted David into his community. He never regretted it for the brigand became a model for everyone; it is even said that later he received the gift of performing miracles, thus witnessing to a truth that history has constantly confirmed: one must never despair of divine mercy.[16]

A sense of humour was yet another pleasing aspect of the life of the Fathers of the Desert. Humour – a simple touch of it at times – could blend itself with the most authentic teaching of the Gospel, as the following apophthegm testifies.

Some brothers came to see Abba Anthony and said, "Give us a word: how can we be saved?" The old man replied, "Do you listen to Scripture? It is very good for you." They resumed, "We want to hear it from you, Father." Then the old man said, "The Gospel prescribes this: If someone strikes you on the right cheek, present him the other." They said, "We cannot do that." "If you cannot present them the other cheek, put up with being struck on one cheek." "We can't do that either." "If you can't do that either," he said, "do not return evil for the evil you have received." They said, "We can't do that either." Then the old man said to his disciple, "Take a small amount of flour and prepare some gruel for them, for they are sick. If you can't do this and won't do that, what can I do for you? You need prayers."[17]

People said that Abba Pambo never smiled. So, one day, the devils, wanting to make him laugh, tied some feathers to a piece of wood and carried these with a show of much strain and effort. When he saw them, Pambo burst out laughing. And the devils said in chorus, "Boo! Boo! Pambo has laughed." But he told them, "I did not laugh, I hold you in contempt for your weakness; it has taken so many of you to carry mere feathers."[18]

Perhaps people in the desert told stories of this nature to "convert" those who did not believe that a sense of humour is almost a Christian virtue and is an excellent criterion of spiritual wholeness.

NOTES

1. The texts quoted are: from St Athanasius, Julian the Apostate and Gibbon. P.F. Anson, *Partir au désert. Vingt siècles d'érémitisme*, Paris, 1967, pp. 29, 67 and 28.
2. L. Renault, *Les Sentences des Pères du désert*, II, 1970, p. 97. For this work, as for those subsequently quoted, see the complete reference in the bibliography.
3. See Acts 2:44-46 and 4:32.
4. See Ex 12:38 and Num 11:4.
5. St Athanasius, *Vie et conduite de notre père Saint Antoine*, Bellefontaine, 1979, p. 33.
6. J.-Cl. Guy, *Les Apophtegmes des Pères du désert*, Bellefontaine, Spiritualité orientale 1, 1966, p. 343.
7. R. Draguet, *Les Pères du désert, textes choisis*, Paris, 1949, pp. 79-80.
8. J.-Cl. Guy, *op. cit.*, p. 181.
9. Palladius, *Les moines du désert: histoire lausiaque*, DDB, Paris, 1981, p. 57.
10. Pl. Deiselle, *Les saints moines d'Orient*, Namur, 1958, pp. 105-106; J.-Cl. Guy, *op. cit.*, p. 120.
11. L. Regnault, *op. cit.*, II, p. 47.
12. *Ibid.*, p. 188.
13. J.-Cl. Guy, *op. cit.*, p. 389.
14. *Ibid.*, p. 405.
15. *Ibid.*, p. 22.
16. Jean Moschus, *Le pré spirituel, op. cit.*, p. 192.
17. J.-Cl. Guy, *op. cit.*, p. 19.
18. *Ibid.*, p. 259.

2

A Christian wisdom

The title of this second chapter presents the Fathers of the Desert as wise men. In what way do they set an example in this domain? We find in them traits of wisdom, the fruit of reflection and experience. Here is a sample of that.

Abba Mark asked Abba Arsenius, "I know a brother who had a few vegetables and who pulled them out (for the purpose of practising greater austerity). Is that right?" Abba Arsenius replied, "Undoubtedly, that is right, but man being what he is, for he has not the strength to practise such austerity, he will soon plant others." We would say: if we do not provide nature with the minimum it needs, it will take some means or other to provide for itself and experience proves it does so generously.[1]

Amma Theodora said, "There was a monk who, because of the great number of temptations he had, wanted to move to some other place. And as he was putting on his sandals, he saw another man beside him who was also putting on his sandals (this was the personalized temptation), and who was telling him, 'You are not leaving because of me for I shall precede you wherever you go.'" We would say: we are what we are no matter where we go; wherever we go we bring along our difficulties; these are an essential part of us.[2]

An elder said: "The one who wishes to live with brothers must not be square but spherical": he must round off the angles.[3]

Another old man said: "The one who loses gold or silver can find some again; the one who wastes time will never recover it."[4] And again: "Wisdom does not consist in speaking but in knowing when to speak. Speak with wisdom, listen before you speak and allow room for an answer; be knowingly ignorant in order to avoid much grief."[5]

This wisdom, however, is obviously neither typically religious nor Christian; the ancient pagan world as well as every other age, had its wise men. There are still wise men and women who teach us how to be a little more human.

We can even say, on the purely human level, that not all the Fathers of the Desert excelled in this respect. Sometimes there were exaggerations; sometimes competitions in ascetic performances came to an unhappy end. Thus we are told of the sad misfortunes of a certain Ptolemy who, eager to be alone with God, came to the point of making solitude an absolute, refusing all contact with men, and even with sacramental life. He finally returned to the world and led a life which was hardly edifying.[6] Anthony was undoubtedly thinking of such cases when he said, "Some have subdued their bodies in asceticism, but for lack of discernment they have fallen away from God."[7]

There were cases when lack of wisdom met with much more serious consequences. Many among the monks of Lower Egypt became involved in doctrinal controversies which shook the Church of the day. We are in the fourth century, in the vicinity of Alexandria. Arius is beginning to spread his doctrine that the Son of God was not eternal but created. This is the heresy of *Arianism* which was condemned by the Nicene Council of 325.

Most of them were not intellectually equipped to enter into the complex and subtle questions then debated. They brought about the fall of many into heresy and finally ruined the monastic life of that region. The polemics which broke the great silence of the desert sometimes degenerated, so they say, into brawls and fights![8]

In short, humanly speaking, the Fathers of the Desert cannot be compared to a gathering of wise men. We must be honest enough to acknowledge that fact. It would be wrong to idealize them.

*

The wisdom they sought with all their might was the one which can be described as *Christian*. Let us clarify this point: Christian wisdom is holiness. In Christianity, the wise man is the saint. This amounts to saying that this wisdom, as we shall see later, will often baffle the wisdom of the world.

Basically, it is founded on the call of God addressed to Abraham and then to his posterity: "Go from your country to the land that I will show you" (cf Gen 12:1). This is a journey for which there are no road maps, no signposts and sometimes no roads. We know where we are going but we have no idea of the details of the journey. In this journey in the night, however, we have infinitely more: we have the Holy Spirit to guide us.

The Fathers of the Desert, in fact, understood that they needed the help of the Spirit, like the blind man who needs someone to accompany him on his road. We are blind in the realm of supernatural life: the Holy Spirit is the light of our eyes.

They would pursue this great adventure under the guidance of the Spirit, more or less successfully, as the case might be. For they would not be moved around like pawns but act as free men who would sometimes meet with resistance. They would experience mishaps on the way, even have serious accidents. Effectively, this would be an *adventure*, not a stage play where everything is planned in advance. The Holy Spirit does not rule out freedom. The more he takes possession of a human being, the more he or she acts responsibly. A certain apophthegm goes like this: "If man wants to, from morning till night, he can become like Christ; and if he wants to, he can also, from morning till night, become like the devil."[9]

The Fathers of the Desert would, therefore, lend themselves as much as possible to the inspiration of the Spirit. The training they received is revealing on that point. When a candidate for life in the desert chose to be a disciple of an elder, the latter, far from indoctrinating his disciple or inculcating ideas and theories in him, would rather seek to liberate him, to free him from clutter, through the practice of obedience, the denial of his self-will in order to enable him to hear the divine voice in the silence of the desert.[10]

For they knew that spiritual formation (which must not be confused with doctrinal formation) bears no comparison with a purely secular formation that has nothing to do with the Spirit. A Christian spiritual master must always remember that he is not the one who forms his disciple, but that his role is to dispose him to receive the lessons of the Other. Here is an apophthegm which shows that the Fathers of the Desert never forgot this essential presence of the Holy Spirit in their lives, and this is a first lesson they teach us on the road to Christian wisdom.

Some brothers came to see Abba John Colobos in order to verify that he did not let his mind wander and did not speak of the mundane matters of his times. They said, "We give thanks to God for the abundant rains of this year, enabling the palm trees to drink their fill and the brothers to find manual work." Abba John told them, "So does the Spirit when he comes down in the heart of humans: they are renewed and they grow leaves in the fear of God."[11]

As it happens at all times, the Holy Spirit was a master who often baffled human reason and, in order to train the Fathers of the Desert in the wisdom which is no longer that of this earth, he sometimes taught them his lessons through intermediaries whom humility alone would allow him to be recognized.

Abba Moses one day said to his brother and disciple Zachary, "Tell me what I must do." At these words, the disciple threw himself at the old man's feet and said, "You are asking that from me, Father?" The old man replied, "Believe me, Zachary my son, I saw the Holy Spirit come down upon you and since then I must consult you."[12]

Abba Arsenius was asking an old Egyptian to give him some spiritual counsel. Another person, who was watching the scene, said, "Abba Arsenius, how can you, having received such a fine Greek and Roman education, speak to this bumpkin?" He replied, "Indeed, I have received a Greek and Roman education but I do not have even the basics of the knowledge this peasant has." He knew, in fact, that the Holy Spirit was speaking through him.[13]

*

Moved by the Spirit and docile to his demands, the Fathers of the Desert would be able to go further on the road to Christian wisdom. It is the wisdom of which St Paul spoke: "Jews demand signs and Greeks desire wisdom [human], but we proclaim Christ crucified, a stumbling block to Jews and foolishness to Gentiles" (1 Cor 1:22-23). It is into the wisdom-folly of the redemption by the cross that they would immerse themselves by performing heroic acts of self-abnegation, and by undergoing the ordeals of life, knowing these other words of Paul:

"All things work together for good for those who love God" (Rom 8:28).

This wisdom made them similar to the witnesses spoken of by the author of the *Letter to the Hebrews*. Like these, although in a different way, we can, in fact, say along with P.F. Anson, "that they went here and there... wandering in deserts, mountains, caverns, the caves of the earth, in search of a better homeland".[14] We can also apply to them this other text from the same Letter to the Hebrews: "You endured a hard struggle with sufferings... you cheerfully accepted the plundering of your possessions, knowing that you yourselves possessed something better and more lasting" (Heb 10:32, 34). Plundering of your possessions... It is not a matter of material goods alone. God sometimes comes like a thief and everything that appeared to be linked to existence seems to collapse. Some trials are all the more painful in that they prevent us from working in the Church in a tangible way. Everything takes place as if God was much more interested in what we are than in what we do.

The Fathers of the Desert knew that one must always travel further along the road of poverty in order to attain Christian wisdom in its fullness. The root of one's being must in some way be reached in order to be purified. We could go on indefinitely telling these delectable stories showing these men and women who seem to have taken sides with God against themselves, and that sometimes to a heroic degree, knowing well that divine victory would ultimately be theirs. An abba used to say, "Even if we are held in absolute contempt in the eyes of men, let us rejoice over the fact that we are honoured in the eyes of God."[15]

It would be interesting to know to what extent Abba Macarius put this maxim into practice in the following circumstance. This famous monk, who had settled near a village, was odiously slandered by a woman of loose

26

morals. "So," he relates, "people took hold of me and dragged me everywhere with soot-covered pans and various objects hanging down from my neck while beating me to the point of death." Subsequently, his innocence was acknowledged and the whole population wanted to come and solemnly apologize. But he, informed about this, fled to some other place.[16]

Another example is that of a nun who, in her community, pretended she was demented so as to be like Christ, mocked and held up to ridicule during his passion.

In her naivety she was putting into practice the words of Scripture: "If you think you are wise in this age, you should become fools" (1 Cor 3:18). She was scorned, spent her time cleaning cauldrons in the kitchen of her monastery. She did not offend anyone, or complain, or say any word against anyone; we are also told that she lived in constant union with God.

Then her holiness was recognized. But when she saw herself become an object of veneration, like Macarius, she fled.[17]

The instances of becoming wise in the eyes of God by appearing as fools in the eyes of the world were many and diverse. A monk from Egypt had settled in a suburb of Constantinople. Having heard of him, the emperor Theodosius II came to visit him incognito. After prayer, the monk invited him to a meal without making any changes in his usual menu for he had nothing else to offer except bread, salt and water. After the meal, which he thought excellent, the emperor revealed his identity and, from that day on, he began to honour the monk: he fled as Abba Macarius and the pseudo-demented nun had done. For he knew, as they did, that such honours might be pitfalls on the way to the wisdom-folly of the cross.[18]

How could the wisdom of the world understand? Already those living at the time of the Fathers of the Desert could be deceived. I have quoted some texts on this sub-

27

ject earlier. Here is another one about a cultured pagan. "These men shun any limelight. They call themselves 'monks' because they want to live in solitude, without any witnesses. They dread the favours of fortune while they fear its setbacks. Could it be that one would deliberately make himself miserable for fear of becoming so? What is this stupid frenzy of minds turned upside down? Perhaps they, being true convicts, inflict upon themselves the punishment they deserve for their crimes. Perhaps their sombre hearts are filled with bitter gall."[19] We could speak, in relation to that and other similar cases, of a totally perverted vision of things if we observed them from the Christian point of view.

We find this "folly" but not only among the Fathers of the Desert but throughout the whole history of the Church. I am thinking of a Curé of Ars or a Charles Borromeo. It still exists today, nor is it limited to priests and religious.

*

But this wisdom-folly leads to Easter; that is its only element of wisdom. By entering into the narrow way of self-abnegation, these Fathers of the Desert lived, body and soul, what St John of the Cross was to describe so well ten centuries later with the help of the image of the log fed into the fire. This log first groans, becomes black, crackles, gets rid of its impurities and there is no beauty in that: then, little by little, it becomes like the fire which is purifying it until it becomes fire itself. For the Holy Spirit does not only guide on the way to wisdom-holiness; he imbues with his own life those who surrender themselves to him.

As this painful purification accomplished its work, the Spirit took possession of these men and women. We are well informed on this subject in the case of St Anthony of whom we have a good biography supplemented by other documents.

After his terrible and triumphant combats against the forces of evil, everything in him was overcome, including his body. Through these excruciating struggles, Anthony had taken part in the passion of Christ; henceforth, he would share, here below, the glory of his resurrection before fully experiencing it in eternity. He had become a *charismatic* in the fullest sense of the word, a permanent receptacle of the Spirit whom he could now give to others.

Human nature, wounded by sin, is restored in him. "This is something to be admired," writes his biographer. "Without having studied letters, he understood and had an insight into everything... He did not have the uncouth manner of a man who grew up in the mountains but he was gracious and courteous. His speech was so seasoned with a divine salt. All those who came to him were disarmed by his charm."[20] As he enumerates his good deeds, the same author bestows upon him the title of "spiritual physician of all Egypt".

We may add that Anthony's radiant influence continued to spread after his death. His influence on the subsequent monastic life – and on Christianity in general – would be extraordinary indeed. "The fact that he was famous everywhere, admired by all, yearned for by all those who had not seen him, is a proof of his virtues and of the loving relationship of his soul with God. Neither writings, nor secular wisdom, nor any art contributed to Anthony's fame except his piety toward God. No one would dare deny that this is a gift of God. How would the renown of this man, huddled and hidden on his mountain, have spread without the hand of God who makes those who belong to him become known everywhere, as he had expressly promised to Anthony at the beginning. These men live in hiding, want to remain hidden, but the Lord shows them to everyone as torches pointing the way..."[21]

At times, this transformation of life was quite physically evident in the Fathers of the Desert. Someone met Abba Sylvanius one day: the latter's face and body were resplendent like those of an angel and the visitor fell on his face. Others were also granted this charism. It was said of Abba Sisoës that, when he was at the point of death, his face shone like the sun.[22]

Let us not be too hasty in thinking that these phenomena are just an edifying literary form. We know, indeed, a similar case, that of Seraphim of Sarov (Russia), almost one of our own times.

He was a hermit of the last century living in a forest in the immediate neighbourhood of his monastery. A layman gave an account of an interview he once had with him. The Father spoke of Christian life, the purpose of which is to acquire the Holy Spirit. The layman, named Motovilov, tells us:

"At one point, Father Seraphim embraced me by the shoulders and held me very tight. Then he said, 'Both of us, you and I, are in the fullness of the Holy Spirit. Why do you not look at me?' 'I cannot look at you, Father. Your face has become brighter than the sun. It hurts my eyes.' The Father then said, 'Have no fear. You too have become as luminous as I am. You are in the fullness of the Holy Spirit. Otherwise, you could not have seen me.'"

Then, Motovilov described what he felt: he was filled with a silence and a peace beyond words, with an extraordinary sweetness and joy. A warmth pervaded through his whole being, while they were in the forest and covered with snow in the middle of winter.

Seraphim of Sarov was first a hermit, then for years a recluse in a cell of his monastery. After struggles known to God alone, he became a charismatic like Anthony the Great. One day, he opened the door of his cell and people came from everywhere to consult him. He invited others to experience joy by calling them "my joy". He had the gift of a supernatural clairvoyance. People have written, "He saw the soul of a man like a face in a mirror *because of the purity of his own spirit.*"[23]

*

Since our purpose is not to observe the Fathers of the Desert as spectators, let us draw some lessons from their wisdom.

First, there is in them a sense of awareness upon which we should reflect, especially nowadays. They lived, in an eminent way, what experience and sheer common sense manage to convince us only with difficulty: this world is but passing, we are in the realm of the relative and the transitory, strangers and travellers on this earth. According to a traditional biblical image, we are, so to speak, in the shepherd's tent, that precarious shelter set up here today, dismantled tomorrow, rolled up, carried away and set up again elsewhere. We could use a yet more modern image, that of the underground. Regular users, who are but a few stations away from their destination, do not bother to settle down.

An abba used to say, "I have been in this desert for a very short time", and when he was asked the meaning of his "very short time", he would reply, "For fifty years." Better yet, these men already considered themselves as dead. One day one of them was told that a close relative of his had died and chosen him as his heir. "His heir?" he said. "But I died before he did!" In a similar circumstance, another had these words to say, "A dead person does not inherit from another dead person!"[24]

The remark made by an abba could help us to understand better and appreciate this state of mind and provide a true explanation for this astonishing telescoping of time: "The whole life of a man is but one day for those who are obsessed with the desire of God."[25]

In order to avoid any misunderstanding, we must hasten to add that this mentality did not make idle, useless parasites of those people. Those who cling to the present life are not necessarily the ones who are the most useful to others. The greatest benefactors of humanity are ultimately the saints, and holiness is not a matter of length of life but of the intensity with which it is lived.

We can say that the Fathers of the Desert made a maximum use of the materials with which future life is unequivocally shaped in the present time: faith, hope and charity.

This profound and living faith in another life which infinitely transcends this one was, as it were, the gateway to their wisdom. The insistence, almost to the point of being an obsession, with which the disciples begged the elders to give them a word "to be saved" stands in contrast with our tendency to make an absolute out of the relative in our present life and, consequently, a relative out of the absolute. Here is an apophthegm which testifies to that and teaches us that the way to thank the disciple for his services consisted in wishing him salvation. Could we think of a better reward? People said that John the Theban, Abba Ammoé's disciple, spent twelve years serving this old man during his illness. But the old man paid no attention to him (a means of testing him according to the methods of formation used by the Fathers of the Desert). Even if he took great pains to serve him, the old man never wished his disciple: "May you be saved." When he was at the point of death and the elders had gathered around him, he took his disciple's hand and said, "Be saved, be saved, be saved!" (a significant repetition). And he entrusted him to the elders saying, "This disciple is an angel, not a man."[26]

*

A second lesson we may draw from the wisdom of these Fathers of the Desert concerns spiritual nourishment. One must eat to survive but each must take the nourishment which suits his nature. One does not give a leaf of lettuce to an animal that feeds on insects, nor a beefsteak to a herbivorous animal. The Christian must also have nourishment adapted to him. Man is an omnivorous animal, it is true, but he needs a well-balanced diet. Let me explain with these two examples.

Some years ago, a rather well-known theologian made a study trip to the United States. It so happened that he spent a few days in a religious community of men. Before his departure, he went to see the superior to take his leave. In a simple and fraternal manner, he made this remark, "What struck me in your community is that we do not feel the kind of atmosphere of prayer and meditation one would expect in a religious order like yours." The superior replied, "Yes, and that is something that worries me."

As they were speaking, the visitor glanced over the top of his desk. There were works in psychoanalysis, psychology, sociology... But one would have searched in vain for a book on spirituality. Some time later he learned that this superior had left the religious life. Perhaps he might have persevered had there been a few religious works as well on his table. His nourishment was not balanced, his spiritual diet was inadequate. And if we ourselves are not well-nourished, we will not be able to nourish others; we can give only what we ourselves possess.

My second example concerns a married woman, a good Christian, who even resorted to spiritual direction. The last time I met her I was surprised to find a change in her. During our conversation, she told me about her growing interest in modern psychology. "Yes," I said, "this science is very much in vogue." This growth of interest was keeping pace with her loss of interest in the so-called mystical theology.

Some years later, I learned that she had lost her faith. There again, a lack of balance in one's nourishment and one topples over. A human being is so fragile! And the most gifted, the most learned, the most brilliant are not necessarily the ones who stand most firm. I can hear the Fathers of the Desert, in all their wisdom, quoting a word from the *Letter to the Hebrews*, not as theoreticians, but because they intensely lived it: "Looking to Jesus..." (Heb 12:2). But they meant the authentic Jesus Christ, not a watered down image of him.

Jesus presented himself under the guise of various symbols: the light, the shepherd, the way... He could also have said, "I am the fixed point." In a world where nothing stands firm, Christ is the one and only fixed point. The one who firmly clings to him by keeping his eyes fixed on him will not topple over.

*

The third lesson, concerning spiritual help, is linked to the preceding one. I said earlier that the disciple adopted the teachings of an elder and obeyed him in all things. However, one cannot strictly speak of an unconditional obedience. He was first advised to choose his master carefully and warned against the illusion of appearances: "The hoary headed old men whose sole merit is derived from their number of years are not necessarily the ones whose footsteps should be followed nor whose doctrine and counsels should be accepted unquestioningly." A danger all the more serious in that the devil (the Fathers of the Desert never forgot his intrusion into every domain, including that of playing the role of a spiritual guide) could use their white hair to deceive the young. "With his prestigious cunning, he loses no time in taking advantage of their (bad) examples to bring about the fall or to ensnare the very ones who, either acting on someone's advice or according to the inclination of their heart, had entered into the way of perfection. Their doctrine and their rules of life become for him a means of leading these poor souls either to a disastrous lukewarm state of soul or to a deadly despair."[27]

Once the master was chosen, the disciple remained responsible for his choice. In this sense, he kept on being vigilant to a certain degree and if his spiritual guide took a wrong turn, he would leave him. He never put his trust in a man who could eventually bring him to his fall.

In quite a number of texts, we see the disciple consulting another abba who would confirm or reject his choice or explain what his elder had told or ordered him to do. An apophthegm gives him this advice: "If you go to question a Father about your thoughts, first pray God and say, 'Lord, put what you wish to say to me on the lips of this elder so that he may tell me. As for myself, I will accept what he will tell me as coming from your lips, Lord. Make him firm in your truth, Lord, so that I may know your will through him as your intermediary.' And thus preserve with care and awe what the Father will say to you."[28]

The elder was also warned: "To instruct one's neighbour is a pitfall for the soul and to wish to raise him in the good nature is a great cause of ruin for the soul. So when you teach your neighbour and tell him, 'Do this or that', look at yourself and think of yourself as picking up a hoe to destroy your house by trying to build that of someone else."[29]

A more than stern warning and even a discouraging one, but better understood if we add the following apophthegm which says that teaching was the function of the Holy Spirit and that the abba was only passing it on, even if he did so through his own human and spiritual experience. Some brothers came to see Abba Felix and begged him to give them a word. But the old man kept silent. After they had begged him for a long time, he told them, "From now on, there are no longer any words. When the brothers used to question the elders and did what they were told, God showed these elders how to speak. But now, since they question without doing what they hear, God has withdrawn the gift of speech from these elders and they no longer find anything to say..."[30]

Obviously, not all the spiritual Fathers had so pessimistic a view. However, in a long litany of self-accusations and beating of his breast – and as he was urging others to do the same – Abba Isaïe had some strong words always worthy of being heard and meditated: "Woe to us who carefully clean up the earth from its thorns, thistles and plants harmful to the fruit trees and who do not carefully clean up our souls... Woe to us, for whereas we have a great need of being trained and educated, we correct the peccadilloes in others."[31]

All authoritarianism was banned as coming from the devil and not from God, and a fair amount of freedom was given to the disciple. A brother was questioning Abba Joseph saying, "I want to leave the monastery and live in solitude." The old man said, "Go wherever you find your soul at peace and unharmed and stay there." The brother replied, "But I am at peace both in the monastery and in a solitary life; what do you want me to do?" The old man said, "If you delight in the peace of both the monastery and life in solitude, place these two thoughts as if on a scale and go wherever you see your thought deriving greater benefit and move on."[32]

They even make us attend what we would call today a life review and it is done without too much regard for people's feelings. Abba Sisoës the Theban said to his disciple, "Tell me what you see in me and I will tell you what I see in you." His disciple replied, "You are kind in your mind but you are somewhat harsh." And the old man retorted, "You are kind but without being kind in your mind."[33]

It is true that, in the writings of the Fathers of the Desert, we find morally dubious attitudes, resulting from ignorance and naivety. But the texts just quoted, and others too, show that we never detect an alienation of the person such as has existed in certain cases very close to us, offshoots of a blind submission to religious leaders who posed as "charismatics" or were considered as such.

The message of these old monks for our times, abounding in gurus of all kinds, could be worded as follows: Seek help in your journey toward God. But remember that you have only one Master, one guide, Christ. "Test the spirits," as Scripture tells us again. See if the one you are freely choosing to guide you does so really in the name of Jesus Christ (cf Mt 23:8-12; 1 Jn 4:1-6).

*

Finally, the fourth lesson. Many of these monks in the desert came from the least refined classes of society. They brought along with them, to the monasteries and hermitages, their uncouth manners, their lack of culture, their simplistic nature. Some texts show them as being naive to an astonishing degree. Do they not tell us of a certain Abba Serapion who broke down in tears and cried out, "They have taken away my God from me!" when he learned that God had no body while he had thought him to be made in his own image. And yet, this same abba was, they tell us, accomplished in the practice of all virtues and most worthy of being recommended because of the austerity of his life.[34]

Fortunately, we are no longer at that stage. Biblical science, in particular, has made astonishing progress. We have become scholars. New methods, such as structuralism, are immediately turned to our benefit for a greater understanding of the Word of God. It is the same in human sciences. One can but rejoice over that.

But if we are far from the simplistic mind of this Abba Serapion and of those like him, are we any holier than they? The lesson of wisdom they teach us is that we must not mistake science for holiness. We must especially not believe that the one can replace the other. We were not told: be learned as your Father in heaven, but, "Be perfect as your heavenly Father is perfect" (Mt 5:48). We possibly have here a small pitfall which could threaten our spiritual life.

If all this knowledge can contribute to make us friends of God, it does not hold the ultimate secret of this friendship. This secret essentially resides in listening attentively to the Spirit, a listening implying obedience in love: to know more, indeed, but in order to love more.

NOTES

1. J.-Cl. Guy, *op. cit.*, p. 34.
2. *Ibid.*, p. 118.
3. *Ibid.*, p. 192.
4. *Ibid.*, p. 370.
5. L. Regnault, *op. cit.*, II, p. 268.
6. Palladius, *op. cit.*, II, p. 91.
7. J.-Cl. Guy, *op. cit.*, p. 21.
8. P. F. Anson, *op. cit.*, pp. 42-44.
9. L. Regnault, *op. cit.*, II, p. 311.
10. Abbot Isaïe, *Recueil ascétique*, Bellefontaine, Spiritualité orientale 7 bis, pp. 19-20.
11. J.-Cl. Guy, *op. cit.*, p. 122.
12. *Ibid.*, p. 99.
13. *Ibid.*, p. 31.
14. P. F. Anson, *op. cit.*, p. 22.
15. J.-Cl. Guy, *op. cit.*, p. 127.
16. *Ibid.*, p. 166.
17. Palladius, *op. cit.*, p. 99. We know that there existed in Russia, and probably still exists, a tradition of people madly in love with Christ: men and women who behaved in the same spirit as this nun.
18. J.-Cl. Guy, *op. cit.*, p. 383.
19. P. F. Anson, *op. cit.*, p. 68.
20. St Athanasius, *op. cit.*, p. 77.
21. *Ibid.*, p. 91

22. J.-Cl. Guy, *op. cit.*, pp. 279 and 291.
23. Seraphim of Sarov, Bellefontaine, 1973, p. 208ff.
24. J.-Cl. Guy, *op. cit.*, p. 156.
25. *Ibid.*, p. 73.
26. *Ibid.*, p. 149.
27. J. Cassian, *Conférences*, II, 13, Cerf (SC), Paris, 1955.
28. L. Regnault, *op. cit.*, II, p. 128.
29. Abbot Isaïe, *op. cit.*, p. 101.
30. J.-Cl. Guy, *op. cit.*, p. 312.
31. Abbot Isaïe, *op. cit.*, p. 37.
32. J.-Cl. Guy, *op. cit.*, p. 142.
33. *Ibid.*, p. 288.
34. J. Cassian, *Conférences*, X, Cerf (SC), Paris, 1955.

3

A liberating ascetism

The ascesis we will deal with in this chapter could be defined briefly as follows: the voluntary denial of things even if good in themselves in view of a greater union with God.

To speak of ascesis is a delicate undertaking, for we are touching a sensitive spot and the persons to whom we address these words always feel more or less under attack.

But can we gloss over this practice of the Fathers of the Desert? Ascesis was such an integral part of their lives that the term practically describes them. They were called *ascetics* and they led an *ascetic* life. There is no authentic Christianity without self-denial. The call to repentance that perpetually echoes throughout the Gospel implies an ascetic self-denial, this one being intimately tied up with sin and its roots in us and, therefore, with our union with God.

In order to show, if need be, that the asceticism practised by the ancient monks is not out-of-date, here are two texts from the Second Vatican Council. In the first one, asceticism is related to personal sanctification; in the second, to the missionary concern of all the faithful.

"Spiritual life is not solely enclosed within participation in liturgy..." Then it speaks of intimate prayer and it goes on: "The Apostle (St Paul) teaches us to bear Jesus' mortification in our body so that the life of Jesus may also manifest itself in our mortal body" (an allusion to the forty-day fast in the desert).

"Through charity, prayer, example and *the efforts of penance*, the ecclesial community exercises a true motherhood in order to lead souls to Christ." We have but to recall certain passages in the Acts of the Apostles: the sending forth of some members in mission is preceded by prayer and *fasting* done by everyone.

In the same sense, during a public audience, Pope Paul VI said: "A Christian life without a spirit of asceticism cannot maintain itself and persevere in fruitful spiritual richness and as an apostolic testimony." Finally the beautiful opening prayer of the Mass for the Tuesday of the first week of Lent must be noted: "Lord, look on us, your children, and grant that our mind, purified by the discipline imposed upon our senses (through asceticism), may be resplendent in your eyes with the desire of finding you."

In order to help us go beyond a first negative impression, we may point out that we are already on familiar grounds. Everybody, in fact, naturally leads an ascetic life. Whether or not we are believers, even if we ignore the word, asceticism is an inherent part of human life in its present condition. If, out of hypocrisy, anyone eluded it, that person would no longer be a man but a human wretch; if he never imposed any acts of self-denial upon himself, he would become the constant plaything of all his whims, of all the latent tendencies in him, of all his instincts, and we can see where that could lead him. We can make an analogous remark about spiritual or mental asceticism. Can we imagine ourselves never exercising any restraint on whatever comes to our minds? There would no longer be any social life.

We put natural asceticism into practice for all sorts of reasons, not all of them being necessarily noble ones. Thus, we will give up having as much food and drink as we would like in order not to harm our health, or pass as gluttons and drunkards; we may do so to keep our figure, or simply for reasons of economy. In the same way, certain professions forbid smoking at work; it is better to go without a few cigarettes than to lose one's job. An employee, who is burning with the desire to tell his boss that he is making life miserable for him, will exercise an ascetic mental self-denial for the sake of his job or a possible promotion.

The examples I have just given show how asceticism is never gratuitous. We give up something of value to ourselves only to acquire something better, even if we are not conscious of this, even if we are mistaken in our priorities, even if we make a thousand detours to achieve our goal. We would readily challenge anyone to prove the contrary. The man who commits suicide does not escape this law which admits no exception: he thinks that giving up life is better for him than to live in suffering or despair.

*

Christian asceticism will obviously be put into practice for an altogether different reason. But before we ask the Fathers of the Desert to define this asceticism and tell us what its purpose is, we should clear up a serious ambiguity. Corporal asceticism does not imply contempt for the body, as opposed to what we sometimes believe and write. Still less is it a matter of "killing" nature. The Fathers of the Desert were too abundantly nourished by the Bible to be oblivious of the texts which state that the work of God is good, even very good. But they also knew that everything in us had fallen more or less into a state of anarchy because of sin. It is therefore a matter of re-establishing order in our faculties. However, there is much more to be said and leaving things stand as they are would not enable us to go beyond the natural level.

Christian tradition affirms the following: through ascetic effort, the body is transformed under the action of the Holy Spirit: the purpose of asceticism is to allow the new life received in baptism to be fully developed. By contributing to this transfiguration of the entire human being into the image of the risen Christ, the ascetic effort acts as a liberating agent in the most profound sense of the word.

Asceticism will contribute toward the purification of the soul. It will reach down to the root of our disarray, of our self-love, of our pride and of our selfishness, so that divine charity may overcome these evil forces in us. An abba used to say: "Love all mortification and your passions will be put down."[1] Cassian, an ancient monastic author already quoted in this book, uses the image of the ploughman removing the brambles and thorns from his field (that is, the ascetic effort) so that his soil, in its restored good condition (that is, the purity of heart), may produce an abundant harvest (that is, the life of union with God, life in the Spirit).[2]

In another passage of his work, the same author establishes a relation between self-abnegation and three books of Scripture, *The Proverbs* which teach man how to lead an honest life; *Ecclesiasticus* which speaks of vanity (we would say inadequacy) of everything that makes up our present life; finally *The Song of Songs* where the soul, purified and united to the Word of God, is already contemplating the realities of heaven.[3] The role of asceticism is thus clearly defined.

*

Fasting (deprivation of food) appears to be a fundamental element of the great Christian tradition of asceticism. "Its goal," writes Placide Deseille, a modern author, "is to transform our appetite for earthly foods into a hunger for God."[4] Can we attempt to set Christian fasting more clearly in its proper place with respect to the practices of other religions? When we are, however so slightly, familiar with the Bible, with the Old Testament in this case, we are struck by the importance and the complexities of the relationship between man and his food. That was probably equally true in other ancient religions. This domain was easily permeated with magic, and taboos played an important role here.

Here is an example presented somewhat as a curiosity but also, and especially, for the purpose of shedding a better light on the change, not to say the revolution, brought about in this domain by Christianity. We find in the *Book of Exodus* a prescription which appears enigmatic to us: "You shall not boil a kid in its mother's milk" (Ex 34:26). Whatever interpretation the Hebrews gave to this text, modern commentators think they can link it with cult practices of the peoples who had previously occupied Palestine; it can be enlightened by certain ways of doing things used some decades ago by some small African tribes. According to these beliefs and practices, one cannot mix just any foods according to one's whims; that is particularly true for meat and milk. Cooking them together is to create an impurity (in the sense that "pure" means unmixed). By eating this food, one assimilates this impurity in oneself, with the pernicious consequences which, one believes, may result from this, particularly sterility. People went so far as to take purges to prevent two substances judged to be opposed to each other from coming in contact in the body.

In this domain as in others, Christianity had a liberating effect.

But there is more to be said. The evangelists give us an account of a controversy between Jesus and the disciples

45

of John the Baptist. The disciples question him about fasting: "Why do we and the Pharisees fast often, but your disciples do not fast?" Jesus replied, "The wedding guests cannot mourn as long as the bridegroom is with them, can they? The days will come when the bridegroom is taken away from them, and then they will fast" (Mt 9:14-15). Then he tells them two parables, very familiar to us, one of which explains that new wine should not be put in old wineskins (cf Mt 9:16-17).

The idea brought out by this text from the Gospel is that fasting takes on a totally new meaning; it is related to the Paschal mystery, a mystery of death and resurrection. Henceforth, whether we eat or whether we fast, we always do so with the purpose of rising to a new life with Christ. We have no doubts that this is the spirit the Fathers of the Desert had when they put this asceticism into practice, even if they did not explicitly and clearly say so.[5]

Corporal asceticism includes other elements too, as the whole life-style of the Fathers of the Desert tells us. It also includes vigils (an area where prudence is more particularly imperative), the rejection of comfort in every form... In short, everything that prevents us from losing touch with reality.

*

To corporal asceticism, the Fathers of the Desert added mental asceticism. In this area, they practised self-denial to a very advanced degree. They spoke of the "vigil of the heart". This last expression is understood in its biblical sense, whereby the heart is not the seat of sentimental feelings but of a profound life. It is in that heart that evil thoughts are born. All efforts, therefore, will consist in preventing this birth of which they do not ignore the disastrous consequences since thoughts move us to words and deeds. The word must therefore not be understood only in its narrow sense but also inasmuch as thought is inseparable from the desires it awakens. "My thinking suggests that I should do this or that..."; the brother often expressed himself in this way when addressing the elder he had come to consult.

"You must constantly watch the head of the serpent," the Fathers used to say, "that is, the first appearance of any thought, and ask it, 'Who are you, where do you come from?'"

Here is a maxim on this subject that goes far and deep: "Keep watch over your eyes and your heart will not see evil things. 'Everyone who looks at [anyone] with lust has already committed adultery' (cf Mt 5:28)."[6] It is no longer a matter of the Gospel precept understood in its literal sense, but of an allusion to the central theme of Scripture, that of the espousal of humanity, of the soul, with God. Any evil thought in which we take delight is like an infidelity to the God whom we love.

But the Fathers of the Desert did not stop there. Evil thoughts had to be dismissed along with the useless ones which could open the way to the former. At the very least, they took the place of the good ones for we are so made that we cannot entertain thoughts about two things at the same time. Neutral in themselves, these thoughts deter us from our conversation with God. The Fathers used to say that they divert us "to the right" as opposed to the evil ones which divert us "to the left". Thus they did violence to themselves, they spoke of their struggle against thoughts.

A brother came to visit an elder, one day, and through the door he could hear a violent quarrel going on. He was most surprised and, thinking that the elder was having a fight with some individual, he went in to stop them. But behold, the abba was alone. He asked him, "Who were you fighting with?" The elder answered, "With my thought. Indeed, I know fourteen books of the Scriptures by heart and when I heard one poor profane word coming from outside when I started my prayer, all these books disappeared and that thought alone would be before me. That is why I was fighting it."[7]

Here is another apophthegm which, in its figurative form, proves the importance the Fathers of the Desert gave to this type of asceticism. One of them said that, one day, some monks were talking about matters related to the soul. One monk had the gift of visions and he saw angels doing honours to them. But when they began to talk about strange (ungodly) things, the angels withdrew and pigs came and wandered about, spreading their foul smell and making a mess everywhere. When the monks again spoke of spiritual matters, the pigs left and the angels returned.[8]

Our old monks also knew that the enemy is never absent from the place. An abba asked God for the grace of falling asleep whenever the conversation would turn to ungodly subjects. For he had noticed that, on the contrary, when they spoke of matters related to God and faith, the tendency was to doze off, whereas trivial matters would awaken everybody.[9]

They had a very well-chosen word to designate harmful or trivial thoughts; they called them "captivities".

One of the most persistent temptations of those living in solitude in these times was to leave their cell. The devil was never short of schemes to achieve his purpose. He was always there tugging at the monk's habit, using the most varied and pious pretexts to entice him to go elsewhere; and, quite often, the inexperienced monk living in solitude would let himself be taken in.

In one apophthegm, two devils meet and one says to the other: "You look very tired." The other replies, "I am exhausted because of the hard work I was given to do. I spend my time moving the monks of Jerusalem to Mount Sinai and those of Mount Sinai to Jerusalem." We could apply this little story to thoughts by completing it as follows: the second devil speaks in his turn and says, "As for me, I am still more exhausted than you are, not because of the weight I must bear but because I have to run constantly. I am busy with only one monk living in solitude. He never leaves his cell but I have to keep moving his thoughts from one place to another."[10]

But we can chase away only what is replaced by something else. The monks were aware of that as these two texts show: "My Father, the abbot Soy of Mount Diolcos told me, 'If thoughts come to the heart of a brother, he cannot turn them absolutely away unless he brings words of the Scriptures or of the elders to his heart. Whenever the master enters his own house, all the strangers there flee away.'"[11]

Abba John says, "I am like a man sitting under a large tree, who sees wild beasts and serpents in large numbers coming to attack him; when he can no longer resist them, he rushes up a tree and is saved. Such am I: I am sitting in my cell and I watch evil thoughts coming against me and, when I have no more strength to fight them, I take refuge in God for prayer and I am saved from the enemy."[12]

Who would dare deny the necessity of this struggle against thoughts or of this mental "sorting out" in order to be united to God? We sense the extent to which this asceticism, with its action of purification – of memory and intelligence – may be a source of unification.

Today, the word "pollution" is in vogue; we speak of the pollution of the air, rivers, etc. Could we not also speak of a mental pollution and of a much needed "spiritual ecology"?

*

The Fathers of the Desert thus lent themselves with courage to the practice of asceticism of mind and body. But if we stopped here, their message would be dangerously thwarted. They can teach us, moreover, that asceticism must be practised with humility and discretion and that we must never lose sight of its aim, which is charity.

Asceticism without humility loses its foundation. It then becomes the worm we ourselves introduce into the fruit. An abba would say, "If you practise asceticism, let not your heart rely on it to keep you but tell your thought: 'Because of the mortification of my body, God is attentive to my misery.' And again, 'Do not rely on your strength, God's help will come.'"[13]

A brother had settled in a village. He fasted so much that people had nicknamed him "the Faster" and he derived a certain amount of gratification from that. An elder named Zeno, who had settled in the neighbouring desert, heard about him and had him come for a visit. The first, no doubt thinking that he would be praised for his fasts, joyfully accepted the invitation. They prayed and sat down. The elder began to work in silence. Since he could not manage to talk with him, the fasting brother was overcome with boredom. So he said, "I want to leave." – "Why?" – "Because I cannot stand this any longer. In the village, I would fast and nothing like this would happen to me." – "In the village", said the elder, "you nourished yourself through your ears. Listen to my advice: do less fasting but do so in secret and all will be well with you."[14]

"If you lead a style of life in which you mortify your body", writes a certain author, "and because of that men admire and honour you, then you must give it up and adopt another style of life so that your labour may not be in vain."[15]

Why did the Fathers of the Desert insist on this relationship between ascetic practices and humility? The enemy here was not pride so much, as we might believe, but what they called "vainglory". It would rather be a matter of vanity. That could surprise us; is not vanity a minor shortcoming, even a ridiculous one and, by that fact, negligible? But then we should ask ourselves why Jesus warned his disciples against the ostentation of the scribes and Pharisees in what precisely concerns asceticism which is exposed to this same shortcoming: seeking to be admired by others. The teaching in the desert rested precisely on these texts of the Gospel.[16]

For our old monks, as for Christ, vanity or vainglory was more serious than it would seem. Here is a test showing that it can, in fact, open the door to other much more dangerous enemies: "What is vainglory? The (exclusive) love of this perishable life, mortification to make your name renowned, a greater love for the glory of men than that of God, being oblivious of what saddens your heart (that is, the knowledge of your innate misery), showing off deeds to be honoured by men and not see the glory of God..."[17] Elsewhere, the same author writes: "I consider that to overcome vainglory and to progress in the knowledge of God is great and honourable; for the one who falls in the shame of passion alienates himself from peace and hardens his heart. It is impossible for the one who loves to be honoured by men to be without passions; jealousy and envy dwell in him."[18]

Asceticism practised with vainglory means that the memory and the desire for God become blurred and even disappear. Fasting thus nourishes self-complacency. The more one fasts, the less one hungers for the true hunger, the hunger for God.

*

One point on which the Fathers of the Desert also insisted is discretion in the practice of asceticism. This insistence shows that this danger was not an illusory one for them. One day, some elders gathered with Anthony the Great and discussed about the best means of growing in perfection. Each one put forth his opinion. Some suggested vigils and fasting, others prayer, solitude, hospitality. Anthony spoke last and declared, "All you have just said, it is true, is necessary for those who thirst for God and wish to reach him. But some unfortunate experiences, of which we have been witnesses, show us that the mother, the guardian, the moderator of all virtues is discretion."[19]

"Excessive fasting harms in the same way as gluttony", writes another author. For they can also bring about excessively lax periods in our spiritual lives. We remember the already quoted text from the same St Anthony: "Some have broken down their body in asceticism, but because they lacked discernment, they fell away from God."[20]

Prayer itself could become an exercise of asceticism. One day, a brother came to see an elder and said, "I have lost my peace for I have learned that a certain woman religious in the village says seven hundred prayers whereas I have been unable to say more than three hundred." "As for me," the old man wisely replied, "for sixty years I have been saying one hundred prayers, as I work for my food and perform the duty of speaking with brothers; as I reflect upon this, I find that I have not been negligent."[21]

What this young brother said is worth noting; he had lost his peace. The criterion of the proper measure is there. Any asceticism of mind or body which is not accompanied by a profound peace is suspicious and even dangerous. We could add that an asceticism is not truly Christian if it does not allow the gifts of the Spirit to shine through, especially those related to relationships with others, such as being amiable and willing to help.

A happy medium must be found which, obviously, is different for each one. Abba Arsenius used to say, "Observe the ships: if they are overburdened with loads that are too heavy, they will sink; if the load is too light, winds will blow them away. If the cargo is moderate, they do not sink nor do winds blow them away. Treat your soul and body fairly; do not subject them to mortifications that are too heavy to bear, else you will no longer be able to cope with a moderate fast." How could one speak with greater wisdom? Here is a pithy expression imbued with the same Christian wisdom: "We have not learned to destroy our body but to destroy our (evil) passions."[22]

One form of asceticism I have not spoken of is what may be called "social fasting". I have already mentioned Abba Ptolemy who reached the point of rejecting any contact with men and who, ultimately, went back into the world and led a life that was hardly edifying.

Discretion, in this form of asceticism as in others, depended on the personal vocation and, by this fact, could be practised to most varied degrees.

Abba Arsenius, whose wise counsel we have just read, was terrifying when the safeguard of his solitude with God was at stake. A lady of high rank, whom he had known at court and who had not hesitated to brave the desert to meet him, found that out at her own expense.

The bishops did not have any more luck. Theophilus, archbishop of Alexandria, came to him one day accompanied by a person of standing. He asked the elder to give him an edifying word. After a short silence, Arsenius replied, "Will you put into practice what I will tell you?" They promised they would. Then the old man told them, "Wherever you know you could find me, stay away from that place."

A monk, who was a stranger, was passing through a neighbouring community and wished to see him. A brother brought him to the elder. The latter gave them such a cool reception that, embarrassed, they quickly took their leave. Then they went to pay a visit to Abba Moses, the former brigand, who greeted them most cordially. When another abba heard of this, he prayed God saying, "Lord, shed some light on this difficulty: one flees company for the sake of your name, the other for the sake of your

53

name welcomes others with open arms." God answered his prayer with a vision of which the meaning seems to be the following: both of them, each in his own way, are equally pleasing to me.[23]

Relationships with women seem to have posed a particular problem. But to what extent can one ignore half of humanity?

Cassian tells us the story of an abba who could not bear to see, not only the face, but even the attire of a woman. One day, by chance, he met a woman on his way; he fled to his monastery "with as much speed and haste as if he had met a lion or a dragon."

God could not have been other than displeased at the sight of such behaviour. He allowed this abba to become totally disabled. Not knowing how to nurse him themselves, the Fathers put him in the care of a convent of nuns. They took charge of him and totally devoted themselves to his care for four years; he died in their arms. We know nothing about his innermost feelings at the time he took leave of this world, and this is most unfortunate. But we may suppose that these sisters had cured him of his phobia.[24]

Some Fathers of the Desert, not so misogynous as he was, might possibly have said, "Neither too much, nor too little." That is the guideline the consecrated celibate may use to adjust the frequency of his relationships with women. And that is being wise, for a certain reserve must be observed in an area where no one is strong. But may we not add the following: there is a wholesome way of considering a person of the other sex, and everything becomes pure for the one who seeks to purify his or her own heart. Besides, is not this relationship necessary to restructure oneself and become a normal human being?

Discretion also implies that one knows how to relax. In the case of the Fathers of the Desert, the weekly Eucharistic meeting was the occasion of sharing a fraternal meal during which cups of wine were passed around. This moment of relaxation allowed them to go then, refreshed, and face the combat in the desert. Those old monks were not oblivious of the counsel of prudence we find in Scripture, "Remember: God is in heaven, while you are on earth."

*

Finally, and here is the most important point, asceticism is oriented to charity; the two must never be opposed in their concrete forms of practice. We must constantly remember that there is one absolute in Christianity: charity. All the rest is but the means. Without the love for God and neighbour, everything is mere words.

An elder said, "Let us acquire the main virtue, charity. Fasting is nothing, a vigil is nothing, any painstaking is nothing in the absence of charity. In fact, it is written: God is charity."[25]

"The Fathers used to say that the devil can imitate us in matters of fasting for he never eats, and what pertains to sleep, for he never sleeps; but he can never imitate humility and charity."[26]

A brother was questioning an abba, "Give me a word; how can one be saved?" The elder replied, "Sit in your cell; if you are hungry, eat; if you are thirsty, drink. There is but one thing, do not speak evil of anyone."[27]

Another abba used to say, "Let us not hurt anyone with our practices of asceticism. Charity comes first and is essential. Charity must remain untouched and is inviolable even if, in such cases, we must give up some of our practices."[28]

Yet another one gives this advice: "If you live with brothers and your thought wants to restrain your food, tell your thought: 'The weak one here is my master.' If you wish to practise abstinence to a greater degree, do it in private, but do not torment your weak brother."[29]

Here is another form of brotherly love which is not always present in our minds, "If your body is weak, do your duty also toward it for fear it might become disabled and force you to ask for your food and be dependent on the one who serves you."[30]

*

The Fathers of the Desert did not only give good advice on this subject; they were not armchair theorists but people who put their teaching into practice. To a visitor who had made him break his fast and was telling him, "I prevented you from being faithful to your rule of fasting", an abba replied, "My rule is above all the precept of charity."

It happened that a hermit, while being visited by a fellow-hermit, broke his fast in order to share his meal with him. Then, as soon as the visitor had left, another came and they started all over again. Thus he had eaten twice even if it meant that he would go three days without taking any food. For these monks held on to both ends of the rope. They knew too well from experience that if charity comes first, asceticism does not become useless for all that and that it could contribute to a growth of love for God and neighbour in the heart of the one who puts it into practice.

"When I receive Christ in your person," an abba used to tell his visitors, "I must restore him; and whatever, out of consideration for him, I relent in my usual eating habits, I will easily compensate by means of a stricter fast." Then he quotes the words of the Lord: "The wedding guests cannot fast while the bridegroom is with them, can they? The days will come when the bridegroom is taken away from them, and then they will fast" (Mk 3:19-20)[31]

This "recuperation" could go far. It is said that when Abba Macarius visited the brothers, he imposed this rule upon himself: "If there is wine, take some because of the brothers, but for every cup you drink, spend a day without drinking any water." The brothers offered him some wine during the meal and the old man accepted with joy. But when his disciple learned this, he told the brothers, "In the name of God, do not offer him any more wine, else he will drive himself to death in his cell."[32]

In the life of Pachomius, whom I have already introduced as the one who organized monastic community life, we find what could be called a pearl on the subject of asceticism related to charity. A bedridden brother, reduced to no more than a skeleton by his illness, asked to have a small chicken for his meal. An unheard-of luxury for a monk! The infirmarians refused to give it to him. When Pachomius heard of this, he reprimanded them and informed them that he himself, who was sick, would take neither food nor drink until they had complied with this brother's wish; this they did. With tears in his eyes, Pachomius quoted these words from Scripture: "To the pure all things are pure" (Titus 1:15). The infirmarians had the letter of the Rule on their side but Pachomius, who had written it, understood the spirit of this Rule.[33]

The same Pachomius also knew how to put charity before asceticism in cases of necessity whenever he was concerned. When he spoke of the trips he usually made on foot during the exhortations he addressed to his monks before he died, he said that he would accept to ride on a donkey whenever he was ill. One must love one's neighbour as oneself as it is said in the Gospel. But if we do not love ourselves much, the neighbour will not be loved either![34]

The exquisite charity which consists in taking a friend's wish into account is not absent from these texts. So it happened that a certain Abba James, who was ill, agreed to discontinue his penitential exercises for a while.[35]

Finally, asceticism and charity are also related to each

other in the sense that we may not judge others by making comparisons between them and what we practise ourselves. Others can do more than we do by doing less. For everything depends on the inspiration of the Holy Spirit, on each one's possibilities and also on one's past life. We have an apophthegm on this subject which can instruct us and incline us to be kind.

A Roman monk had settled in the desert. Another abba came to visit him one day to become acquainted with him and to talk about matters pertaining to the spiritual life. When the visitor entered his hut, he was surprised to find a bed (monks slept on mere mats) and there was even a blanket and a small pillow. Moreover, here was something hardly believable; this monk had a servant who cooked for him whereas cooked meals were considered to be a luxury, incompatible with the style of life in the desert.

The Roman man had noticed his visitor's astonishment. After their spiritual conversation, he asked him, "What did you do before you became a monk?" "I watched over animals." "You slept in a bed?" "No, shepherds sleep on the ground." "You had someone to serve you?" "Obviously not." "You did some cooking?" "No, shepherds eat whatever they can find near at hand." "Ah, well, you see," resumed the Roman, "in Rome, I was a person of rank. I slept in a magnificent bed and now I have but this wretched and mean bed. I had many slaves at my service and now I have only this man. I had splendid meals prepared for me and here I eat a few vegetables. In the course of these meals, there were singers, men and women, musicians, and now I rise during the night to recite a few psalms. And in addition to all that, my health is not very good." Then the former shepherd said, "I was somewhat too hasty in judging you. In fact, your asceticism is much more austere than mine in spite of appearances. As for me, hardly anything has changed in comparison with the past and now

I even lead a more gentle life than I did before. You have more merit than I do."[36]

*

More than fifteen centuries after the period of the Fathers of the Desert, there lived a famous man, Giorgio La Pira, the mayor of Florence, an admirable Christian. Like the young brothers with respect to the elderly monks, many people came to consult him and asked for advice or for an edifying word.

One day, a wealthy American lady came to see him and admitted she suffered from the emptiness of her life: she was bored and disgusted with everything. As she was speaking, she lit up a very expensive cigarette. "How many cigarettes do you smoke in a day?" La Pira asked her. "Many." "You could perhaps cut the number by half and give the value of this half to the poor." "Oh!" she replied, "I could very well give the full value without depriving myself for all that!" – "No," he insisted, "the price of that half!"

She had the wisdom of heeding his advice and of putting this asceticism into practice, for that is what all this was about. This marked a new beginning for her. She again found joy in life, the joy that always comes with the gift of oneself. A gift that costs little, that remains external to ourselves, will never bring a profound joy.

The joy of living. We must extend the expression and speak of the joy of living with God even if, to be sure, it does not exclude other joys. To the effort in asceticism may be applied the words of the psalmist: "Those who sow in tears reap with shouts of joy" (Ps 126:5) provided the asceticism is fully assumed and not simply put up with, and for that, the motivation must be strong. And also the parable of the treasure hidden in a field. The one who finds it goes in his joy and sells all he has to give all that he is (cf Mt 13:44).

Through the importance they gave to asceticism, the Fathers of the Desert hand down a message that is always applicable to our times. An austere message, no doubt, demanding a generous effort on the part of the one who wants to put it into practice but which is certainly not regretted afterwards. "Let no one abuse you," one of them used to say as he summed it all; "in the same way that the earth cannot bear fruit on its own without seed and water, so it is impossible for man to bear fruit without the labour of asceticism."[37]

NOTES

1. Abbot Isaïe, *op. cit.*, p. 105.
2. J. Cassian, *Conferences*, I, 4, *op. cit.*
3. *Ibid.*, III, 6.
4. Pl. Deseille, "Guide spirituel" in *Collectanea Cisterciensia*, 1969, p. 300.
5. In this perspective, what is to be thought of the hunger strikes and fast often carried out to a heroic degree by men and women who are not always believers as forms of protest against the injustices in society? It seems impossible to think that they are not, although indirectly, part of the mystery of redemption.
6. Abbot Isaïe, *op. cit.*, p. 134.
7. J.-Cl. Guy, *op. cit.*, p. 359.
8. *Ibid.*, p. 400.
9. *Ibid.*, p. 155.
10. L. Regnault, *op. cit.*, II, p. 244.
11. *Ibid.*, p. 306.
12. J.-Cl. Guy, *op. cit.*, p. 122.
13. Abbot Isaïe, *op. cit.*, p. 60.
14. J.-Cl. Guy, *op. cit.*, p. 98.
15. Abbot Isaïe, *op. cit.*, p. 62.
16. Cf Mt 6:1-6.
17. Abbot Isaïe, *op. cit.*, p. 260.
18. *Ibid.*, p. 145.
19. J. Cassian, *Conferences*, II, 4, *op. cit.*
20. J.-Cl. Guy, *op. cit.*, p. 21.
21. Palladius, *op. cit.*, pp. 76-77.
22. J.-Cl. Guy, *op. cit.*, p. 256.
23. *Ibid.*, pp. 36, 31, 42.
24. J. Cassian, *Conferences*, VII, 26, *op. cit.*
25. L. Regnault, *Nouveau recueil, op. cit.*, p. 99.
26. *Ibid.*, p. 99.

27. J.-Cl. Guy, *op. cit.*, p. 144.
28. J. Cassian, *Conferences*, I, 7, *op. cit.*
29. Abbot Isaïe, *op. cit.*, pp. 78-79.
30. L. Regnault, *op. cit.*, II, p. 99.
31. Pl. Deseille, *Les saints moines d'Orient*, Namur, 1958, p. 117.
32. J.-Cl. Guy, *op. cit.*, p. 172.
33. R. Draguet, *Les Pères du désert*, Paris, 1949, p. 107.
34. *Ibid.*, p. 117.
35. *Ibid.*, p. 171.
36. J.-Cl. Guy, *op. cit.*, p. 271.
37. Abbot Isaïe, *op. cit.*, p. 66.

4

An incessant prayer

To speak of the prayer of the Fathers of the Desert amounts to listening to them speak of prayer. It is also watching them pray.

You should not imagine them kneeling on prie-dieux or before the Blessed Sacrament; nor in a more modern posture: sitting on a hassock in front of an icon cleverly lit up in candlelight to create a mystical ambience. No, you must visualize them more often than not seated in their cell, busy plaiting cords, weaving baskets, mats, which they would sell in the markets of Alexandria or elsewhere. That was the kind of work they would do while incessantly repeating a particular verse from the psalms or an invocation drawn from or inspired by Scripture.

"While performing my manual tasks," Abba Lucius used to say, "I pray unceasingly. I sit down with God, moistening my rushes or plaiting my cords and saying, 'Have mercy on me, God, in your great kindness, and in keeping with the greatness of your compassion, take away my sin!'"[1]

Obviously, they prayed also at times other than those devoted to manual labour. A spiritual master gives this advice: "Already in the morning, sit on a low stool, enter totally into your heart and stay there. And so, bent over in an uncomfortable position in a spirit of penance, you will cry out with perseverance: 'Lord Jesus Christ, have mercy on me.'"[2]

The concepts of monastic life and the ways of leading it might have been markedly different: life in solitude is one thing, the coexistence of brothers in a community is another. Nevertheless, this ideal of incessant prayer is found everywhere in ancient monasticism like a constant and a nostalgia as well, a kind of interiorized desire. St Basil, who put a strong emphasis on community life, nevertheless, kept up the ideal of the continuous prayer of the hermits. "While our hands are at work," he writes, "we can praise God with psalms, hymns and spiritual songs; either on our lips, when that is possible and edifying, or at least in our hearts. Else, how could we reconcile these two ideas of St Paul: pray unceasingly and labour without respite."[3] "Among the things prescribed to us," Pachomius was wont to say, "there is the incessant prayer."

Here are two maxims which testify to this desire of praying constantly. They give us the impression of being thumbnail biographies and we can appreciate their beauty: "Force yourself to say numerous prayers during the night, for prayer is the light of your soul."[4]

In spiritual life, the word "night" can hold many meanings. "Love to pray incessantly so that your heart may be enlightened."[5]

Thus, prayer was not "programmed". God is everywhere, so must prayer be. God is always there, so with prayer. There were "intense moments" of prayer, the liturgical offices, for instance, but they were like the arches of a bridge: they sustained a continuous prayer.

Cassian even perceives incessant prayer as the purpose of monastic life and he detects its effects: "The whole purpose of the monk consists in an uninterrupted perseverance in prayer. Inasmuch as it is possible for human frailty, it is an effort to attain a tranquil stillness of the soul and a perpetual purity."[6] Like asceticism, and along with it, prayer contributes to the purification of the heart.

The whole life of these men and women thus unfolded against a resonant background of prayerful existence. They spoke of God incessantly and we could say that they heard God constantly speaking to them in the sense that they had the Scriptures always present in their mind, of which they had memorized entire books, especially the psalter. The Bible was the voice of their prayer.

Undoubtedly, this prayer did not always limit itself to one sole invocation and it could be expressed in most elaborate forms. However, its particular trait is always simplicity, for it was rooted in the Bible. Biblical prayer, in fact, is simple, trusting, naive in the best sense of the word: natural with nothing artificial about it. We could give you many examples of this.

An abba used to say, "Do not pose as learned people in the wording of your prayer for often only childlike stammerings, simple and unadorned, are what have honoured our Father in heaven. Do not undertake to say heaps of words for fear that your mind may wander in its search for words."

But prayer is an ongoing reality. Indeed, it takes on a new name in their texts – we could expect that to happen: *contemplation*. The monk has ruminated his humble and simple prayer so much that it has gradually transformed itself. Henceforth, the prayer casts his eyes on God and can no longer turn away.

We have been watching the Fathers of the Desert sitting in their cell, working while repeating this or that verse from Scripture. Now their prayer, becoming still simpler, has kindled itself. Indeed, it rises like a flame and with such force that it carries the prayer up with itself. If we still want to see this prayer, we must raise our head for, according to the words of Cassian, he is "like the tight-rope dancer"; he is somewhere between heaven and earth.[7]

At this stage, if the monk still has distractions, these are reversed. A camel-driver came by one day to pick up a bundle of ropes from Abba John Colobos. The abba went into his dwelling to fetch them and forgot about him, his mind being set on God. The camel-driver then disturbed him again as he knocked on his door. Again Abba John came out, went in... and forgot. The camel-driver knocked a third time, the old monk came out, then went in repeating: "Ropes, camel, ropes, camel..." And so he managed to remember.[8]

An abba came to visit another abba. The latter cooked lentils for him and said, "Let us make a short prayer first." This "short" prayer, in fact, lasted all night and, come morning, the visitor left and both forgot all about eating the dish of lentils.[9]

One must note that this prayer of the Fathers of the Desert is *Christian*. For, obviously, prayer is a natural religious phenomenon which existed among the pagans. We are told, for instance, that during an ecstasy Abba Poemen saw Mary at the foot of Jesus' cross and shed tears with her.[10] These men and women were not oblivious of the role of the Holy Spirit in their prayer. "The Spirit helps us in our weakness," wrote St Paul, "for we do not know how to pray as we ought, but that very Spirit intercedes with sighs too deep for words. And God, who searches the heart, knows what is the mind of the Spirit, because the Spirit intercedes for the saints according to the will of God" (Rom 8:26-27).

Isaac the Syrian wrote these magnificent words on this subject: "When the Spirit establishes his abode in a human being, this person can no longer stop praying, for the Spirit prays unceasingly in him or her. Whether he or she is sleeping or keeping vigil, prayer no longer leaves the soul. The movements of the purified spirit are mute voices which chant psalms in secret to the invisible."[11]

Cassian writes at length about the prayer of the Fathers

of the Desert becoming increasingly purified and we find expressions from his pen which, ten centuries later, make us think of what a St John of the Cross and a St Teresa of Avila would say. They call this contemplation "the prayer of fire". "It is, as it were, beyond expression. It reaches out beyond all human feelings. It is neither the sound of the voice nor the movements of the tongue nor articulated words. The soul, bathed in light from on high, no longer uses human speech, which is always inadequate. Like an overabundant spring, all feelings overflow and spring forth toward God at the same time. *In this short moment*, it says so many things that the soul, once it has recovered itself, could neither express nor go over them in its memory."[12] It is already something of the life to come experienced here below.

Evidently, this is enough to discourage us if we have not in the least reached that point. However, I have noted these few words in Cassian's text: "in this short moment" and in the text by Isaac the Syrian quoted above, it is clearly said: "in the one whose spirit is *purified*".

Other testimonies show us that if these summits of prayer were sometimes reached – and we have no reason to doubt that they were – our monks, in fact, were still really down to earth and the contemplation of sublime and heavenly realities could still alternate with moments when they clashed with earthly realities. Abba Macarius the Alexandrian tells us the following: "Once I wanted to keep my mind concentrated on God for only five days. The decision being made, I shut my cell and my yard so that I would not have to see to anyone and, standing, I started on Monday. I gave this directive to my mind: 'Do not come down from heaven! You have there the angels, the archangels, the powers from above.' I held on for two full days, but I made the devil so furious that he took the form of fire and flames and burned everything I had in my cell; even the mat on which I lay was consumed by fire and I thought I was completely roasted myself! Finally, I took fright and gave up on the third day. I had not been able to keep my mind focused."[13]

Elsewhere, writers speak of darts with which the devil, always lying in wait, wanted to pierce the monk, especially when he was praying.[14] An old account shows us devils bent on disturbing the prayers in this way. They would come and gently pull down their eyelids to put them to sleep; the devils would put their fingers in their mouths to make them yawn...[15]

But they have many other tricks up their sleeves! This is shown in other accounts which must not always be taken literally but which, nonetheless, show the extreme importance the Fathers of the Desert gave to incessant prayer. An abba tells us: "One day, while I was in my cell, doing manual work and praying at the same time, I saw a devil come in through the window. He had the shape of a small child and he began to dance in front of me. Then he said, 'Monk, do I dance well?' I made no answer. He resumed, 'My dance is not pleasing to you?' As I was answering absolutely nothing, he said, 'Evil monk! You think you are doing something important! I am telling you that you deceived yourself when you read a certain verse of a psalm'"[16]

An abba, although zealous at prayer, had fallen asleep from fatigue. A devil close by was keeping watch over him with the attentive care of a most devoted nurse, carefully seeing that nothing or no one came to trouble his sleep. For he well knew that, once awake, the monk would immediately go back to his praise of God and that he, by the very fact, would be chased away.

In a text related to the life of prayer, an abba said, "When one penetrates deep into the desert, he must take along with him faith, hope and charity. His mind must be well made up and he must be firmly determined to achieve his goal. For combats will besiege him from every side."

These words are not aimed only at distractions during prayer of which I will speak later. In the teaching of this spiritual master, as in the naive accounts I have just recalled, there is the symbol of an altogether deeper struggle. In our present condition, indeed, whether we are explaining things as we wish or as we can, we are not spontaneously turned to God.

Our prayer is our constant relationship with the Lord. But it is like the thread that is cut with scissors. We reestablish the communication but the scissors are always there, never tired of working and they are handled by invisible hands; we do not quite know to whom or what they belong.

The devils have changed aspect. Do they come to close our eyelids when we want to pray? It would seem that in our modern world, they rather seek to blind our eyes so that God may completely disappear from our sight.

These hostile powers are also interior. The Fathers of the Desert were familiar with the dreaded *acedia*, a word designating a reality which is also not unknown to us, even if we ignore this word which is difficult to analyze. Acedia means boredom with the things of God, a kind of distaste for everything concerning the spiritual life, a kind of discouragement.

Cassian has sketched the portrait of the monk who has become a prey to acedia: "There he is. He feels exhausted, is always out of his cell, watches out for a brother who might eventually visit him, is tempted to visit one himself. He watches the course of the sun which is much too slow for him. He feels that his style of life has no meaning, no value..."[17]

In short, if we want to do more than just address a few words to God from time to time and follow the example of these Fathers of the Desert who were great pray-ers, who were living and constant prayers themselves as much as this is possible here below, we must put up a struggle.

*

The Fathers of the Desert waged this war of prayer with courage, generosity and perseverance. They used weapons to this effect, weapons they turned against themselves in order to destroy in them what was an obstacle to the union with God, a union they wanted to be as profound, as intimate, as constant, as conscious as possible. There are plenty of texts that speak of this violence we must exercise against ourselves. "I have been wearing the habit for seventy years," says Abba Theodorus, "and not a single day have I been at rest." And in another apophthegm, it is said, "No one may receive the seal of the Holy Spirit without undergoing afflictions and fatigues."

Among the weapons, there is one called *recollection*. Prayer implies and requires interior recollection. Recollection means that the mind isolates itself from the outside world – something which can be achieved in the midst of a crowd – in order to concentrate itself on its interior life, the place for an encounter with God.

The Fathers of the Desert had no illusions about this point as about many others. They knew that no interior silence was possible unless one practised the vigil of the senses. Our senses are the doors which open out onto noisy and busy streets – onto a world whose logic is questionable as we well know: the logic of the imaginary projecting us as much into the past as into the future, or into the unreal. We must close both doors and windows. An abba used to say, "Be the gatekeeper of your heart so that no stranger may come in and so that, whenever someone comes near and knocks on your door, you may be able to say: 'Are you one of us or one of our enemies?'"

There is no lack of edifying examples of this in the apophthegms. Abba Isidore one day went to visit Abba Theophilus, archbishop of Alexandria, and when he returned to Scete, the brothers asked him, "How is the city?" But he said, "Indeed brothers, I did not see anyone's face except that of the archbishop." When they heard that, the brothers were filled with anxiety and said, "Was there any disaster, Abba?" He replied, "Not at all, but the thought of watching anyone did not get the best of me." At these words, they were filled with admiration and resolved to restrain their eyes from indulging in wandering.[18]

At times, the lesson was still more direct. Abba Arsenius one day came to a place where there were reeds swaying in the wind. And the elder asked the brothers, "What is that motion?" The young brothers fell straightaway into the trap and answered, "Reeds". Then the old man said to them, "If anyone remains recollected and then hears the song of a small bird, his heart will not savour the same kind of peace. How it is so for you who are subjected to the swaying of these reeds!"[19]

Here are two more apophthegms which, this time, feature some Mothers of the Desert. An amma was travelling with other nuns when she met a monk. When he caught sight of them, he made a detour. Then the amma told him, "If you were a true monk, you would not have even noticed that we were women."[20]

It is said that, for sixty years, Amma Sarah lived near the river (the Nile) and not once did she turn around to have a look at it.[21]

Is all that but exaggeration? To be sure, that is obvious. But this is done intentionally. When the Fathers of the Desert used these edifying stories in the formation of their disciples to a life of prayer, they showed that they had a good knowledge of human nature, that it is inclined to become despondent. If the principles are not very lofty, what will the tangible achievements be like?

We often find this advice in the apophthegms: "Keep to your cell, it will teach you all things," that is, do not go and disperse yourself but remain recollected. Keep to your cell in that sense, it will teach you to pray.

Another weapon used in the struggle for prayer was *openness of heart*. Disciples were advised to disclose all the evil thoughts that troubled their souls to their spiritual Father. The Fathers of the Desert knew, as well as modern psychologists, that our thoughts are living things, that they work within ourselves.

An elder used to say, "In the same way that the tropical creepers entwine themselves around the tree and choke out the fruit, that the worm eats its way into wood, moths in clothing, and rust the iron, so does sin consume and stifle the one who does not disclose it."[22]

And another one: "An evil thought exposed to light immediately loses its venom. Even before the Father has passed judgement, the formidable serpent, from whose dark and subterranean lair, the confession, so to speak, has snatched the thought away, projected it in light and shown off its shame as a spectacle, hastens to retreat. What he suggests has a hold over us only inasmuch as it remains hidden in the bottom of our heart."[23]

The relation to the life of prayer is very obvious: if we allow this obscure world of evil to proliferate, to gnaw its way into our spiritual life, it will put up a screen between God and ourselves.

But the openness of heart among the Fathers of the Desert did not consist only in disclosing one's evil thoughts; it also fostered what we call spiritual companionship. The elder was not "used only as a garbage bin", as we say; through his charism of discernment of spirits, he helped his brother make constant progress in his life of union with God, in his life of prayer.

With the same kind of exaggeration and for the same reasons as for recollection, Abba Anthony used to say, "To the extent that this is possible, the monk must confide to the elders the number of steps he makes and the number of drops of water he drinks in his cell in order to know whether or not he is deceiving himself in that."[24]

Another weapon, hidden under the dust of ages but considered to be awesome by the Fathers of the Desert, was *compunction*. A high-sounding, worn-out word indeed, which nevertheless describes a fundamentally Christian interior attitude.

Compunction (to puncture means to prick) is the acute uncomfortable feeling springing from our condition as sinners. But we must hasten to add: sinners forgiven, loved and redeemed, else we would have to speak rather of despair. Compunction, in short, is the Holy Week including Easter Sunday, that we always carry within ourselves.

What characterizes this feeling is its depth and, consequently, its stability; for it is always and everywhere true that we are forgiven sinners. The exterior fluctuations of our sensitivity cannot shake off compunction. It is like the bottom of the sea forever calm in spite of terrifying storms on its surface. It is something of eternity with its everlasting character that has entered into the heart of the one who is imbued with it. We can sense this feeling as we watch modern saints like Charles de Foucauld or the Curé of Ars. Their face is at peace and something of the light of Mount Tabor flashes in their eyes; they experience the Paschal mystery to an intense degree.

The Fathers of the Desert were well aware that this feeling of compunction is a fertile ground in which prayer may grow, the true Christian prayer which, whatever forms it may take, is always rooted in the mystery of the death and resurrection of Christ.

Here is one of their prayers, nourished with the sap of compunction: "You possess strength, mercy, help, protection, forgiveness and patience; for who am I in the hands of ten evil ones from whom you have saved me? I have nothing to offer you for I am a sinner and unworthy of your gifts, and you have kept me from the hands of my enemies. But you are my Lord and my God, and yours is the glory, protection, mercy, help and power."[25]

The pastors of the Church point out today how the sense of sin is weakening among Christians. By the same token, forgiveness has no longer any meaning and prayer loses a good part of its role as nourishment.

Like all the gifts of God, compunction has the power of its origin. However, because it is offered to the liberty of man, it can become as feeble as a child. If it possesses the beauty of the flower, it shares its fragile nature. That is expressed in a certain text with the help of another image: "Compunction is a small burning lamp; if you do not protect it carefully, it suddenly goes out. Excess of food blows it out, prolonged sleep stifles it, slander makes it disappear, so does gossip..."[26]

Fraternal charity is also part of this arsenal in the desert. "How," says Cassian as he recalls Matthew 5:23-24, "can we offer our prayers to God if a brother holds something against us?" All the more reason, if we hold something against him. Besides, the hurt that charity experiences would quickly call things to order. Abba Nilus says, "Everything you do to take revenge against a brother who has done you harm will come back to you at the time of prayer." And he adds, "Everything you will have borne out of love, you will find its fruit at the time of prayer."[27]

*

After this necessarily incomplete inventory of the instruments of combat, here are a few reflections drawn from the experience of the Fathers of the Desert. First, three definitions.

First definition: Prayer is not something but someone. Prayer is God and the one who is praying. If the pray-er passes completely into his prayer – and only then is it truly prayer – how could God not completely pass into the acceptance of it! This shows the personal character of prayer in an eminent way.

Today, more than in the past, we like to pray together as evidenced by the existence of numerous prayer groups, and one can only rejoice about that. But clearly, group prayer must never take the place of personal prayer. It must rather intensify it. Besides, what would praying together mean if we have not met the personal God in the intimacy of our heart?

The Fathers of the Desert had clearly understood the relationship between group and personal prayer. They show this in the way they celebrated the divine office as a group: they alternated psalms with moments of silence set aside for a more intimate dialogue with the Lord.

Second definition: Prayer is prayer! Some could say, "Prayer, why, it is to be with the brothers, sharing the great intentions of the world!" No! All that is a part of prayer only when inserted into our intimate relationship with God. Similarly, we sometimes say, "Work is prayer." No, work is work and prayer is prayer. Let us call things by their proper names. Work can be a part of prayer depending on the spirit in which it is done, but in itself it is distinct from prayer.

The Fathers of the Desert did not confuse the two. They prayed while they worked, as we have seen. They even chose, as much as possible, the kinds of work which allowed them to pray more easily. But never would they have said, "Let us limit ourselves to work, our work will take the place of prayer." Such a mentality can conceal an escape, a failure. It is sometimes easier to move about much, to get in touch with people, than to remain before God in prayer, in faith.

Third definition: The prayer of a Christian must be Christian. Prayer is first and foremost a natural religious initiative which needs to be christianized.

The Fathers of the Desert always knew how to keep their prayer within the vast context of the mystery of the salvation in Jesus Christ. This was true about their most intimate prayer, as we have seen when speaking about compunction, since the prayer that flows from it takes its roots in the mystery of the death and resurrection of Jesus, the heart of Christianity as well as the heart of our lives.

That was also true, to be sure, about the liturgical prayer which makes us relive the history of salvation all through the year. Thus the office of Terce (nine in the morning) was related to the descent of the Holy Spirit on the Apostles; that of Sext (noon), the death of the Lord on the cross to save humankind. That of None (3 p.m.) with what, in the Creed, we call the descent into hell where Christ definitely broke open the gates of death. The office of Vespers corresponded to the evening offering of a sacrificed lamb in the Old Covenant. But it obviously took on a new meaning; those who celebrated it knew who the real victim was and it called for our act of thanksgiving.

As for the morning office called Lauds (praise), "These verses we sing every day," writes Cassian, "justify us for doing so: *'My God, my God, I meditate on you in the watches of the night'* (Ps 63:6); *'In the morning, my prayer comes before you'* (Ps 88:13); *'I rise before dawn and cry for help'* (Ps 119:147); *'My eyes are awake before each watch of the night, that I may meditate on your promise'* (Ps 119:148). But we can also detect here the joyful celebration of his rising from the grave on Easter morning."[28]

Their prayer for humankind was not separated from the mystery of salvation. Nowadays, people pray much more for the poor, for the victims of social injustice... The Fathers of the Desert prayed for these same intentions. But they knew that the poorest in the Church are the sinners, the wealthy with a hardened heart, the executioners. We narrow down the Gospel message and we partly de-christianize our prayer if we see only the first. Jesus has not forgotten them, and we must pray for them. But the latter are also loved of God who wants them to be saved; and we must assume responsibility for them.

*

At the beginning of this chapter, we saw the Fathers of the Desert relentlessly repeating an expression drawn from or inspired by Scripture. St Augustine was aware of this practice since he wrote: "People say that in Egypt the brothers say frequent but very short prayers which, as it were, are rapidly sent up to heaven."

Abba Isaac, albeit reluctantly, reveals his invocation to passing visitors, a "secret of prayer". It is drawn from Psalm 71: *O my God, come to my aid, make haste to help me!* It is a simple appeal for help and it is of such importance, he explains at length, that it is the answer to all spiritual needs and helps to drive away all the temptations which assail the monk.[29]

Is this verse as efficacious as Abba Isaac seems to think? However it may be, if the effect is not always tangible, it is certainly profound. It establishes an intimacy with God, and we always end up by being like the one we habitually live with.

Consider the *Jesus Prayer* of the Eastern Church: "Lord Jesus Christ, Son of the living God, have mercy on me, a sinner." We too can adopt it and make it our continual prayer.

The Fathers of the Desert could not have better described the fruits of incessant prayer than with an apophthegm featuring a devil sent on mission, obviously with evil intent. When he arrived at a certain monk's dwelling, he remained fixed at the same spot for ten days, unable to move ahead, for the monk was incessantly praying day and night. He thus returned empty-handed to the one who had sent him.[30]

It is very obvious that we can adopt other forms of prayer, better adapted to our religious sensitivity. We can find them in the psalter, that astonishing anthology of the Old Testament in which man's cry to God is heard and is applicable to every circumstance and need of life. We can also find them, to be sure, in the New Testament, especially in the Gospels.

When sung, this refined form of the word can intervene and play an important role in helping to create a good obsession. Singing invocations, even to secular melodies in vogue, is certainly not out of place. St Louis-Marie Grignion of Montfort, the outstanding missionary of France during the seventeenth century, made people sing hymns he composed in this way.

This prayer of a single invocation, repeated indefinitely, is obviously not the only form possible. Here we are in a domain where the proper thing to do is to be particularly attentive to the promptings of the Holy Spirit. A large number of Christians, partly thanks to prayer, have achieved a profound union with God without putting into practice nor even knowing about this method of praying.

We must try to pray incessantly and, therefore, everywhere. But we must know how to set aside for ourselves moments more especially devoted to this intimate dialogue with God. People sometimes have preferences about the place for these "moments of intensity". While these preferences may be naturally justified, they may also come from the Holy Spirit. God is everywhere. However, he provides places for us to meet him and we must respond to them. Why this place rather than another? He is the one who knows.

But we may possibly have some false ideas about prayer and gauge its value and effectiveness from its "tangible" effects. Prayer is above all an act of faith. The purpose of all the means the Fathers of the Desert used was not to create emotions within themselves, but to intensify this act of faith which is somewhat the soul of prayer.

Our life is very different from that of the Fathers of the Desert. Our occupations are not the same and, in general, they do not allow us to turn easily to God for any length of time. But if many things have changed since these early times, the principal source of inspiration for Christian prayer is always there, always true to himself: the Holy Spirit. He is the one who makes our poor desire to pray bear fruit.

For the lesson we may glean from the Fathers of the Desert concerns especially the intimate dispositions which allow the Holy Spirit to do his work. Even if the exhortation to "pray incessantly" always remained for them an ideal which they never fully realised, they strove with all their might to attain it. Whatever our state of life, our occupations and the exterior ambience may be, there are always moments when restraint of the eye and tongue is possible, as well as the rejection of trivial thoughts which ruin and impede the action of the Spirit. If we do whatever we can, God will do the rest, and that "rest" may be what is most important.

*

As a conclusion to this chapter, I would like to say a few words about distractions in prayer.

The Fathers of the Desert knew of these instances when the Spirit took full possession of them so that distractions became impossible or their effect was reversed. These, however, were but transitory mystical states and the works of the imagination were anything but unknown to them.

A brother came to tell an elder, "Many strange thoughts come to my mind." The elder replied, "Take in a deep breath and hold it for an indefinite length of time." "I can't do that." "If you cannot do that, neither can you prevent distractions."[31]

Distractions cannot be avoided in our present condition, but there is no cause for alarm. For the one who deliberately turns to God, distractions are but a purely superficial phenomenon. They are the cloud passing in front of the sun.

In another apophthegm, a brother was telling an elder, "My thoughts wander and this grieves me." The elder replied, "Remain recollected and your thoughts will come back to the essential. Indeed, in the same way, the jenny is tied down while its colt runs here and there but always comes back to its mother wherever she is. So it is with the thoughts of the one who persists in remaining near God; even if they wander, they always come back."[32] He could have added: "When you become aware that you have distractions, come back to God immediately, simply, calmly, and do not especially dwell on them for they are snares laid out against your life of prayer. You would thus be binding yourself to a dead past while it is in the present moment of life that the Lord is making his rendezvous with you."

But I think we must go further yet. St Paul says that "all things work together for good for those who love God" (Rom 8:38). Why should distractions in prayer – obviously inasmuch as we do not take delight in them – not be included in this "all things"?

My monastery publishes a periodical on spirituality: *Ecoute* (Listen). One day, while preparing a plate, the brother who prints it accidentally spilled a drop of a corrosive substance on a picture and damaged it beyond repair. However, once it was printed, we had a surprise. We could see that the consequences of this damage were the best we could have hoped for: a hole in the sky, a hole which could be the sun lighting up a landscape.

Is there not a symbol of some worth here with respect to distractions in prayer? But that is not all. It can also be applied to all the negative aspects of our existence: our failures, blunders, even our sins. Nothing is lost, but everything helps to shed a mysterious light on our life even if this light actually belongs to the realm of faith.

How could the love of God, which gives prayer its ultimate meaning, be better expressed? And if the Fathers of the Desert aspired to pray incessantly, it was in order to respond, in the best way they could, to this love which they knew was waiting on them.

NOTES

1. J.-Cl. Guy, *op. cit.*, p. 162.
2. Pl. Deseille, *Guide spirituel*, *op. cit.*, p. 302.
3. *Ibid.*, p. 303.
4. Abbot Isaïe, *op. cit.*, p. 56.
5. *Ibid.*, p. 129.
6. J. Cassian, *Conferences*, IX, 2, *op. cit.*
7. Id., *Conferences*, XXIII, 9. Quoted by R. Draguet, *op. cit.*, p. XLIX.
8. J.-Cl. Guy, *op. cit.*, p. 129.
9. L. Regnault, *Les Sentences...*, *Série des anonymes*, Solesmes – Bellefontaine, 1985, p. 58.
10. J.-Cl. Guy, *op. cit.*, p. 246.
11. Pl. Deseille, *Guide spirituel*, *op. cit.*, p. 282.
12. J. Cassian, *Conferences*, IX, 25, *op. cit.*
13. Palladius, *op. cit.*, p. 70.
14. Pl. Deseille, *Les saint moines...*, *op. cit.*, p. 92.
15. L. Regnault, *op. cit.*, II, p. 202.
16. John Moschus, *Le Pré spirituel*, *op. cit.*, p. 213.
17. Pl. Deseille, *Les saints moines...*, *op. cit.*, p. 127.
18. J.-Cl. Guy, *op. cit.*, p. 135.
19. *Ibid.*, p. 35.
20. L. Regnault, *op. cit.*, p. 59.
21. J.-Cl. Guy, *op. cit.*, p. 298.
22. Abbot Isaïe, *op. cit.*, p. 297.
23. J. Cassian, *Conferences*, II, 10, *op. cit.*
24. J.-Cl. Guy, *op. cit.*, p. 29.

25. Abbot Isaïe, *op. cit.*, p. 113.
26. Pl. Deseille, *op. cit.*, p. 282.
27. J.-Cl. Guy, *op. cit.*, p. 202.
28. Pl. Deseille, *op. cit.*, pp. 90-97. According to the Roman way of calculating the time of day, *Terce* was the third hour of the day, *Sext* the sixth, *None* the ninth. Vespers came from Vesper, the first star to appear in the sky.
29. J. Cassian, *Conferences*, X, 9-14.
30. L. Regnault, *op. cit.*, p. 136.
31. J.-Cl. Guy, *op. cit.*, p. 223.
32. *Ibid.*, p. 347.

5

An effective charity

We can affirm straightaway that the charity of the Fathers of the Desert challenges our times marked by violence, harshness, inhumanity to our fellow beings. In fact, we shall see how those men and women, quite coarse by nature, could manage to perform acts of such thoughtfulness toward others that they confound us today, fifteen centuries later.

And that was because they surrendered their lives to the action of the Holy Spirit who, as St Paul reminds us, pours into our hearts gifts like gentleness, patience, willingness to serve others, kindness, faithfulness, self-control and generosity (cf Gal 5:22-23). The texts we could quote are almost countless.

Many of these first monks were hermits. Thus, by definition, they lived in solitude. But this solitude was not an absolute. There can exist vocations for a complete solitude or for an almost complete one. Then charity toward neighbour is exercised through prayer, a life of penance, because of the mysterious reality of faith called the communion of saints. For the Fathers of the Desert, however, this was not usually the case, and their contacts with their colleagues, though rare, were enough to allow them to put into practice, in concrete actions, the Lord's commandment: "Love one another". Moreover, they often led a common life with one or even several disciples.

Besides, these hermits came together every week for the Eucharist. This gathering also provided the possibility for them to practise charity among themselves. Obviously, this was not a problem for monks living in community.

"Some brothers do not limit themselves to the only services prescribed by the Rule," writes Cassian. "They sometimes get up in the night stealthily to perform the tasks of others and thus give them some relief." We can appreciate still better the value of this service when we think how parsimoniously the time allotted to sleep was calculated. Did not Abba Arsenius say that one hour's sleep was enough for the monk if he was a good fighter? An extreme case, undoubtedly, not to say an imaginary one, which lets us understand, however, that the tendency was not to sleep late in the morning.[1]

Here are other examples of thoughtfulness in the practice of charity which would appear excessive to us.

Two brothers were performing the same kind of task, one being very skilful with his hands, the other much less so. Sometimes the latter could not manage to be successful in making the object he was working at. In order that his clumsy companion might not feel humiliated, the first, from time to time, would deliberately not make a success of his either.

It is said that a brother had made some baskets and was fastening on the handles when he heard his neighbour say, "What shall I do? The market day will soon be here and I have no handles to put on my baskets." Then he loosened the handles of his own baskets and brought them to the brother saying, "Here, I have these extra ones; take them and put them on your baskets."[2]

Some elders came to see Abba Poemen and said, "If we see some brothers dozing off at prayer, would you want us to reprimand them?" He replied, "As for myself, whenever I see a brother falling asleep, I put his head on my knees and let him rest."[3]

Here is an apophthegm that shows how a difficult problem can be solved in charity. It was said that, from the beginning, Abba Zeno never accepted anything from anyone. Those who brought him things were distressed by the fact that he refused to accept anything. On the other hand, others would come to Zeno hoping to receive some souvenir from this outstanding elder and he had nothing to give them. These would also return home distressed. The elder said to himself, "What shall I do since those who bring me things are hurt as much as those who wish to receive something? Here is what seems good to me: if anyone brings me anything, I'll accept it and I'll give it to the one who asks me for something." By doing this, he was at peace and made everyone happy.[4]

Hospitality was a special opportunity for the Fathers of the Desert to pour on others the love of God which filled their souls. A text offers some advice about this: "If the brother is a stranger, feeble and wearing dirty clothes, wash them for him. If they are torn, mend them... If he is in need, do not send him off empty-handed, but give him some of the blessings God has lavished upon you, knowing that what you have is not your own but a gift from God."[5]

Let us also listen to the advice given to brothers who travel: "If you are travelling along with a brother older than you are, do not have him carry the baggage. But if both of you are young, carry it a little way each in turn and let the one burdened with the baggage walk ahead. If you are travelling along together and one of you is weak, let him walk ahead so that he may take a rest when he wishes."[6]

Such advice is still precious for us, especially if we understand the expression "travelling along together" in its figurative sense. When we accompany others on the road of life, it happens that we move too fast without giving too much consideration to those who are struggling to follow us. And we even treat them harshly sometimes assuming that they are as strong as we are. And still, they too sometimes have heavy burdens to carry of which we are unaware, whereas an attentive charity should make us sense this.

We are struck, on the other hand, by the importance given in these old texts to what we call good breeding, courtesy or good manners. The Fathers of the Desert knew how to say "Good day", "Thank you", "Please", "Sorry". And, undoubtedly, this was so because they already knew how to say these things to God. They can teach us how to christianize these humble virtues practised in our contacts with others by investing them with the plenitude of Christian charity. And, first and foremost, they can help us not to forget these virtues. Is it by chance that in the distant times of faith they become blurred? When God disappears from our sight, selfishness takes the upper hand and the beastly dimensions of man rise to the surface again.

And what about kindliness, a virtue so difficult to put into practice? A council meeting was held against a brother, and Abba Moses was invited to it. He refused to attend. The priest sent someone to tell him, "Come, everybody is waiting for you." So he rose and left. But he took along a jug with a hole in it, filled it with water and carried it on his back. The others, coming out to meet him, asked him, "What is that, Father?" The abba replied, "My sins are flowing out behind me and I do not see them, and I am coming here today to pass judgement on the sin of another!" When they heard him, they said nothing to the brother and forgave him.[7]

A brother who had committed a sin was driven out of the church. Abba Bessarion stood up and joined him saying, "I too am a sinner."[8]

But they do more than make a symbolic gesture. Thus we quite often see some monks who, although innocent, do penance with their brother sinners or even in their stead.

To kindliness, one could add mutual support, no less difficult to practise. Here is an apophthegm on this subject which, in a deliberately harsh way, points out its necessity, not only for the sake of peace in community, which would not amount to much, but to make us come out of our egoistic self-centredness and liberate the powers of love within us.

Abba Anoub and his six brothers decided to lead a monastic life together. They settled down in an old temple in which there was a large stone statue. Every morning of the first week, the old man stood up and stoned the face of the statue and every evening he said to the statue, "Forgive me!" And he did so every day. On Saturday, his brothers asked him, "Does a sensible man act this way?" "This," Abba Anoub replied, "I did because of you. When you saw me stone the statue, did it speak or was it annoyed?" "No." "And again, when I asked it to forgive me, did it say, 'I will not forgive you'?" "No." "Well," said the elder, "if you want us to live together, let us become like this statue. Else, there are four doors in this temple, let each one go his own way." They all stayed. They benefited from the lesson and lived together in peace.[9]

An abba used to say, "Put up with every man as God puts up with you."[10] There was no lack of opportunities... An abba met another one who was carrying a deceased brother. He said, "That is good of you to bear the dead, but you would do still better if you bore up with the living."[11]

These people, devoted to silence, were not oblivious of the sins of the tongue, and charity toward neighbour sometimes consisted in suggesting edifying examples and in giving advice, always useful to us.

An elder used to say, "When we met together at first, we used to speak of things that were of help to the soul, and we would become better and rise to heaven. Now, we meet to fall into slander and we pull each other down into the abyss..."[12]

Prevention is better than cure. "When a brother comes to visit you," said an elder, "do not give free rein to your heart but especially pray in secret for, at that moment, you have everything to fear because of slander."[13] The Fathers of the Desert knew that the enemy is particularly active in that field. For, "when a brother visits another," it is again said, "the devil of slander either precedes or accompanies him."[14]

A brother came to visit the famous Abba Macarius. After prayer, he said to the elder, "Father, it is now forty years since I stopped eating meat, and I am still tempted by it." The elder replied, "Don't say that to me but, I pray you, tell me: How many days have you spent without slandering your brother, without judging your neighbour?" The brother bowed down his head and said, "Pray for me, Father, so that I may begin."[15]

The author of the *Letter of St James* has reminded us, moreover, that the most difficult asceticism to practise is that of the tongue; the one who masters that tiny little instrument is a perfect man. The Fathers of the Desert could have left us an apophthegm of this type: "If the body is destined to be totally transfigured, the tongue will be the last to be so, and not without some difficulty!"

But, according to them, what does God think of slander? An abba (described as a saint) learned that one of his brothers had fallen into sin and said, "He has done wrong." A few days later, the brother died and an angel came with the brother's soul to see the abba and said, "Here, the one you have slandered has died. Where do you want me to throw him? Into the Kingdom or into the fires of hell?" The elder, in tears, asked God to forgive him this sin.[16]

Judging others is usurping a power that belongs to God alone. According to sound logic, this function should be carried out to the end. The elders used to say, "The one who allows himself to accuse his neighbour acts like the one who pulls the legislator or the judge from his seat and wants to judge in his place, as if he were accusing and denouncing his weakness. So it amounts to a rebellion of the servant against his Lord and against the Judge of the living and the dead."[17]

Another form of charity. These old monks knew how to avoid being narrow-minded in the practice of their observances. A brother came to see Abba Poemen during Lent to expose his thoughts to him. Then he said, "I very nearly abstained myself from coming here today." The old man asked him why. The brother resumed, "I said to myself: perhaps he will not welcome me because it is Lent." Abba Poemen then said, "We have not learned to shut the door made of wood but rather the door of our tongue."[18]

Charity was also manifested in the desert in the form of spiritual counsels. "Give me a word (to be saved)", this is how the brother approached the elder. The latter spoke and the brother would return home edified, bringing with him a maxim to meditate, an example to imitate. As a rule, the abba would not make a speech but he would pronounce one word which came not so much from his head as from his heart.

These spiritual companions sometimes exercised this ministry with an inexhaustible patience. A brother, absent-minded by nature, came to see Abba John Colobos and questioned him. Having received a word from him, he went back to his cell and forgot what the old man had said. He came back and heard the same word... and forgot it. This happened several times and, finally, he did not dare question Abba John again. Later, when he met him, he said, "Do you know, Abba, that I have again forgotten what you told me? But in order not to burden you, I did not come." Then the elder had someone light a lamp, then other lamps were lit from the first and he asked, "Has this lamp suffered any loss by the fact that it was used to light the others?" He replied, "No." The elder resumed, "So is it for John: even if every one of the inhabitants of the desert came to see me, they would not turn me away from the charity of Christ."[19]

It sometimes happened that, for very precise reasons, the abba would refuse to answer. A brother came to see Abba Theodorus and spent three days begging him to give him a living word but he received no answer. He left very distressed. Then the elder's disciple said to him, "Why did you not give him a living word? He was very dejected when he left." The elder replied, "Indeed, I did not speak to him for he is a beginner who seeks to glorify himself with the words of others."[20]

The abba knew, from this help from spiritual counsel, that he was at the service of the friendship between God and his brothers; a friendship about which God is earnest and demands a reciprocal response. To put this message across to a visitor who might have forgotten it was again a way of practising fraternal charity.

Going to see an elder to receive from him a beautiful teaching did not necessarily imply an exchange of words. Three brothers were in the habit of seeing Abba Anthony every year. Two of them once questioned him about their thoughts and the salvation of their soul, but the third always kept silent. After a long time, Abba Anthony said to him, "You have been coming now for such a long time, and you ask me no questions." The other replied, "One thing alone is enough for me, Father, and that is to see you."[21] In another text, it is said, "Even if he does not buy anything, the one who enters into a perfumery can enjoy the pleasant scent. So it is for the one who visits the Fathers."[22]

Most of the monks whom people came to see were not priests. Because of this, they may have something to teach us in an indirect way, at a time when every member of the people of God is urged to fulfil the role which suits him or her best in the Church. For, in their eyes, spiritual counsel was a charism of the Spirit, not necessarily linked to ministerial priesthood, even if, obviously, the priest is particularly enabled to fulfil this role.

Abba Joseph tells us, "When we were sitting with Abba Poemen, he referred to Agathon as abba." And we said to him, "He is very young. Why do you call him abba?" And Abba Poemen replied, "Because of his mouth, he must be called abba."[23]

The Spirit can give this charism to a youth, as was the case here. We can believe that he also gives it to more mature persons whose human and spiritual experience he then uses. Of course, we do not launch ourselves into this activity without due consideration. Besides, one could find poor counsellors among the Fathers of the Desert, and Cassian, as we have seen, warned people against this possibility. But if we must not be too hasty about believing that we are invested with a role as a spiritual director of some importance, circumstances, nevertheless, can lead us to help our brothers in that domain. If anyone, prompted by the Spirit, comes to speak to us about his own spiritual life, we should not be too quick to think and say that it is of no concern to us.

We have just seen with what patience those counsellors knew how to listen. One form of poverty of which our times suffer and which we never sufficiently emphasize is precisely the inability to listen, a trait in striking contrast with the excessive number of words which surround us.

That there should be men and women able to welcome their brothers and listen to them is an essential need in our present world, provided that *listening* is synonymous with *loving*, implying how forgetting oneself can be difficult.

If "beggars" of this type come to us, we will not always immediately see the profound, often hidden, reason for this and we will be tempted to think that they take up our time. Still, devoting one's time to others is also giving one's life to God. Cardinal Mercier spoke of "the charity of the ear" in connection with this. Love of neighbour among the Fathers of the Desert was not a weakness. We have already seen this in Abba Theodorus' attitude.

We find texts in the apophthegms that teach us good lessons on this, always with the touch of humour that makes them easier to accept and remember.

A young brother arrived in a community. Seeing his brothers at work, he said, "You work here?" "Yes, and don't you work?" "No, I am like Mary of Bethany at the feet of the Lord; I meditate, read, pray, I am a spiritual man." They gave him a cell with a book and left him there. Time went by and he began to feel hungry. He decided to go out and wander around in the kitchen area. He happened to meet an abba. "Haven't the brothers eaten already?" he asked. "Yes, a long time ago." "Why didn't you tell me?" "Because you are a spiritual man. You pray all the time, you are above these earthly necessities. We, on the other hand, still have to eat to live, and so we have to work."[24]

It is said that, when he was young, John Colobos one day said to his older brother with whom he was leading a monastic life, "I would like to be free from all worry, like the angels who do not work but who constantly pay homage to God." He left for the desert. After a week, he came back to his brother. When he knocked on the door, he heard his brother call out, "Who are you?" He replied, "I am John, your brother." And the other answered, "John has become an angel, he is no longer among men." And John begged him saying, "I am truly your brother!" And he did not open the door but left him there in his distress until morning. Then, as he opened the door for him, he said, "You are a man and you must start working again for your food."[25]

A brother came to see Abba Theodorus and began to talk about things he had never yet put into practice. The old man said to him, "You have not yet found the ship nor loaded its cargo, and before having sailed, there you are already in the city. Perform works first, then you can give us speeches the way you are doing now."[26]

A brother came to see Abba Sylvanius and expressed his intention of taking revenge against someone who had done him harm. Then he said to the elder, "Let us say a prayer together." They stood up and recited the *Our Father*. But Abba Sylvanius altered it in this way, "Do not forgive us our trespasses as we do not forgive those who trespass against us." The brother retorted, "Not like that, Father." "Yes. Sylvanius does not say any other prayer for you." Then the brother forgave his enemy.[27]

We could cite any number of such examples.

If we must know how to practise charity toward others in that way, we must also know how to appreciate it if we benefit by it. In the two texts about the young brothers who did not want to work we are told that they humbled themselves and asked to be forgiven.

*

Up until now, we have observed the Fathers of the Desert practising charity toward their neighbour. But the neighbour was... another Father of the desert. Was this not then a kind of "selfish" charity practised within these groups of two, ten, a hundred?

We have criticized them harshly in the past. We have perceived their retreat as a kind of "helter-skelter flight", an escape motivated by an attitude of indifference with respect to the rest of humankind. Worse than that: a certain contempt.

That they were very concerned about their personal salvation, who could hold that against them without being Pharisaic? To desire God and to aspire to be happy is not to be selfish, it is to go in the direction of one's ultimate goal. This desire for God must be purified. But we can think that it undergoes a "purification on its own". The more we have this desire, the less room there is for self-ishness; and we all the more desire salvation and happi-ness for others. This certainly was the case for the Fathers of the Desert. Whereas, on the contrary, it is not evident that the one who has little concern for his own salvation would have much more for that of others.

Sometimes, it is true, to the question: "How can one be saved?" the given response is: "Flee from man." But these monks, even if there may have been some exceptions, are not misanthropes, far from it! If there is a flight, it would perhaps be more proper to speak of a "forward flight" or a vertical one. In Christianity, one can move forward only by going upward. And we would like to bring others along.

To desire God is to love him, and the true love of God never closes itself to others, its inclination being, on the contrary, to open itself ever more to all. It is impossible that these men and women in the desert, who had left everything for God, would not, by the very fact, have been drawn toward other humans, although in a different way. On this subject, they have left us a most evocative image, that of the circle. God is at the centre; the rays converging from the circumference toward the centre are human beings. The closer a ray comes to the centre, the closer it is to the other rays.

How could they not have loved their fellow beings since they allowed themselves to be imbued by the Holy Spirit who is a Spirit of love? One of them, undoubtedly speaking from his own experience, said, "Those who are filled with the Holy Spirit groan and lament about humankind, imploring God for all of Adam's posterity. If they are moaning and in tears, it is because they are aflame with the love of the Spirit for humanity. Then the Spirit brings on in them such a joy and such an enthusiasm for charity that, were it possible, they would enclose everyone in their heart making no distinctions between the good and the bad."[28]

Faithful to St Paul's recommendations, they make prayers of petition for peace in the world, for persons they know, for those in authority, etc.

We shall now see how they found practical expressions when it was a matter of loving a neighbour other than the monk.

Cassian says of the Fathers of Egypt that, thanks to their labour, they gathered large quantities of food and directed it either to areas subjected to famine or to those who languished in prisons.[29]

And we can also add their fasts to the list. For if fasting, as I have said, helps to detach ourselves from the earth, enkindles a hunger for God and makes one more disposed to the action of the Holy Spirit, it enabled them also to accumulate savings which they used for the benefit of others. Besides, that is a traditional ultimate purpose of fasting in the Church and in monasticism, and it always remains a worthy one. An abba used to say, "In order to feed the poor, it is good to go so far as to deprive oneself of food."[30]

Trips to the city to sell the produce of their labour could offer them the opportunity of practising charity. This was how Abba Agathon met a sick stranger, lying in the public square with no one to take care of him. The elder rented an apartment and stayed with him, doing manual labour to pay the rent and spending the remainder of his money for his own needs and those of the sick man. He stayed there four months, until the stranger was well again. Then he went back in peace to his solitude. The same Abba Agathon used to say, "If I could meet a victim of leprosy, give him my body in exchange for his, I would be very happy."[31] Who could find a better way of describing charity?

We are told of an abba who sold himself several times as a slave in order to convert his masters. Even if this example cannot be imitated, it shows how far true love of neighbour can go.

Another Father's way of doing things reveals one of the secrets of this charity. He gave to the poor but never in person. He would deposit his offering at some place and the recipient would pick it up. One day, he was asked why he acted that way. He replied, "Because I am not the one who gives, God is the one giving through me." More precisely, he was saying, "The Virgin Mary is the one giving through me."[32] (This shows that Marian devotion goes back further than we sometimes think.)

Charity does not consist only in giving but also in the way we give. An old man said, "When you give alms out of fear of God, do not give it coldly and harshly, but look at the poor with a joyful soul and a gentle expression on your face, and thus raise him with honour above yourself, knowing that the offering to the poor is the treasure of Christ and that the Lord loves the one who gives with joy."[33]

Not only in business affairs can the Fathers of the Desert be our masters today. Obviously, our complex economic system was unknown to them. But they can help us acquire a genuine Christian spirit in an area where we can easily be harsh. Feelings have no place in business, as the saying goes; they would be out of place. And it is true that avoiding this harshness is often difficult.

The Fathers of the Desert were businessmen in the sense that they sold the fruit of their labour themselves, in the markets of the neighbouring towns, and they purchased consumer goods as we all do. But they disliked bargaining. They did not seek to make as much money as possible. In their deals, they conformed to an example from on high since one of them used to say, "God sells salvation to those who want to buy it at a very low price: a small piece of bread, a coat of no value, a glass of fresh water, an offering..."[34]

According to the testimony of those who knew him, whenever he had to purchase something at the market, Abba Agathon would look around in order to pick out one particular person selling his or her ware. If he happened to see some widow who appeared to be in financial straits and who had the object he was trying to find, he would say to her, "How much do you sell that for?" He would give whatever she asked; but if he did not have enough money, he would say, "Please, forgive me."[35]

A brother went to see a widow to buy some linen. While she was attending to him, she sighed. The brother asked her, "What is the matter?" The widow replied, "God sent you here today so that our children may have something to eat." When he heard these words, the brother felt sorry for her and he stealthily put the linen he had bought back into the widow's supply.[36]

I think we could say this: For them, whether they were purchasing or selling, the partner was, above all, never someone they would use to make money, but a brother to meet and to love in the Lord. That is essential and must be the basis of business for a Christian. Practically speaking, we then do the best we can. But we must never lose sight of this basis. This principle, which allows us to do business according to the heart of God, also creates peace.

Always remain at peace. That is the point constantly made in the apophthegms which deal with purchases and sales. Peace rather than money: such could have been the motto of the Fathers of the Desert in this domain. It is said that when Abba Amoun sold an object, he indicated the price only once and accepted whatever he was given in silence and in peace. Likewise, when he wanted to purchase an object, he gave the indicated price in silence and took the object without adding a word.[37]

A brother was questioning an elder: "What should I do, for I am in trouble when I sell the work of my hands?" The old man replied, "Say the price of each object once, then if you think you could lower it somewhat, do so; then you will find rest (peace)."[38]

As for the skirmishes with thieves, there are some stories which must not always be taken literally, nor re-enacted in case of robbery. Nevertheless, they give us an idea of the sense of priorities the Fathers of the Desert had. When some offenders arrived unexpectedly at the time of the liturgical office, the superior told the brothers, "Let us allow them to do their work, and, as for us, let us do ours."[39]

One of the most reliable criteria of the authenticity of the charity toward the neighbour is the risk we take in practising it. Anthony the Great would not hesitate to leave his solitude and go to Alexandria to help martyrs, confound heretics or convert pagans. All that, evidently, was not done without being exposed to danger.

Risking one's life out of love for others requires courage. To compromise one's reputation requires a greater courage perhaps. The Fathers of the Desert did this occasionally: we see them visiting prostitutes in the hope of bringing them back to God. Here we must tell the beautiful story of Paesia, the repentant sinner.

This young girl had become a benefactor of the Fathers by offering them her house as a pied-à-terre whenever they went to the city. One day, they learned that Paesia had fallen in her ways and very badly so! "She was charitable to us," they said, "it is now our turn to help her and go to her aid." One of them, John Colobos, went to see her in her room and said, "What have you got against Jesus that you should have come to this?" Then he began to weep. Disturbed, she asked, "Is it possible to do penance?" "Yes", he replied. Then she told him, "Take me wherever you wish." They left. He was probably thinking of entrusting her to a monastery of nuns but she died on the way in the desert and God made Abba John understand that one hour of repentance had been enough for her to become agreeable in God's sight again.[40]

*

The love we have for God is proved by our effective charity toward our brother. St John recalls that in his first letter; "Those who say, 'I love God', and hate their brothers or sisters, are liars" (1 Jn 4:20). The Fathers of the Desert were far from incurring this reproach. But can we not love God and show our love for him in a more direct, more personal way? They teach us that this is also possible.

Love aspires to presence. The Fathers of the Desert cultivated this presence of God as much as human nature permitted. "If we seek God," an abba used to say, "he will manifest himself to us; if we hold him back, he will stay close to us."[41] And another one, "Like the emperor's soldiers who, when they stand at attention, cannot look to the right or left, so is it with man if he remains in the presence of God."[42]

This last apophthegm also suggests that to love God is to be a person of fidelity. Some brothers came to see Abba Agathon to put him to the test. They said to him, "Are you this Agathon who people say is a sinner?" "Yes, I am the one," he replied. They went on, "You are Agathon the proud?" "Yes, I am he." "Are you the one who constantly talks about trivial matters?" "Yes, I am he." "Are you Agathon, the heretic?" "No," he said. "I am not a heretic." Then they asked him, "Tell us why you have accepted all the abuse we heaped upon you and now you reject this last accusation." He replied, "The first accusations, I make to myself and they are even useful to my soul. But heresy separates one from God, and I do not want to be separated from God."[43]

Here is another apophthegm no less revealing. An elder said, "Put your effort and care so as not to offend God who dwells in you." When we more or less consciously think of sin, we spontaneously look at ourselves and wonder what drawbacks and what advantages would result for us from the fact of sinning or of not sinning. Here, we first look at God and what matters above all is not to offend him; and that is the very criterion of the love we have for him.[44]

God was "first served". They did not leave him out in the waiting-room when alien thoughts insisted on being heard. The vigil of the heart (the sorting out of thoughts) was an essential practice for them as we have seen in the chapter on prayer.

When we love someone, we naturally offer gifts to that person. The Fathers of the Desert knew it was possible to show one's love to a person without for all that giving him or her material things that were not needed or that they did not have. They did the same with God for whom they had thoughtful and considerate attentions which confound us today. They knew how to offer him what was not in the category of the useful but certainly agreeable; and that was their response to the gift of redemption. Abba Poemen used to say that every night Abba Isidore would weave a bundle of palms. The brothers urged him saying, "Rest a while for you are getting on in years." But he would reply, "Even if someone burned Isidore and scattered his ashes in the wind, there would be no rest for me because the Son of God came here to save us."[45]

To love God means to listen to him attentively. When a child says to an adult, "You are not listening to me", he means: you do not love me. He knows very well that

100

indifference is the opposite of love. Who has not undergone the painful experience of speaking to someone who is not listening? We give of ourselves in what we say and we aspire to being accepted; that is a definition of true love. God also gave himself in his Word and he wants to be accepted. The Fathers of the Desert knew that very well and they would have endorsed John of the Cross without any hesitation when he writes one millennium later: "God uttered but one Word, his Son. He says it over and over in an eternal silence: the soul must listen to him (love him) in silence."

Be silent in order to listen, to love. But without forgetting the classical distinction between being silent and being mute. A few years ago, when I was still living in the monastery, I received the visit of a man one day, an official who was coming for a purely administrative matter. The matter being settled, he said, "I would like to ask you a question: I am totally ignorant about monastic life, this is the first time I come inside a monastery. But my wife, who knows a little about this, told me, 'You know, you are wasting your time for he will not say one single word in reply; monks never speak.'"

I explained to him that monks are silent not mute; being mute is exactly the opposite of being silent. Mutism is a wall. A mute person does not speak but neither does he hear. Silence is the pre-requisite for listening. When a professor demands silence in his classroom, it is not to have mute people in front of him but attentive students.

To listen to God also means to obey him, and this means to love him. It is a way, as an abba used to say, of manifesting our love to God by "intermingling our will with his". We could not find a better definition for Christian obedience.

When we love someone, we admire what that person does; conversely, indifference toward the works testifies to an indifference – therefore, a lack of love – for their author. Did the Fathers of the Desert manifest their love for God in their contemplative admiration of creation? We must admit that we have few texts on that subject. But that does not necessarily run counter to our statement. All the more so that they knew the psalms of praise which are inspired by the works of creation. We are told that someone was astonished by the fact that St Anthony had few books. He replied, "Nature is my book, and I can read it when I wish, it is always available."

And here we have a delightful apophthegm which goes in that direction. The brothers of Abba Poemen said, "Let us leave this place, for the neighbouring monasteries disturb us and we are losing our souls; see, we even hear little children who prevent us from having inner peace." Abba Poemen said, "Is it because of angels' voices that you want to leave here?"[46]

A text from Cassian illustrates this idea: "We know God through the splendours of his creation. When we think that he has counted the grains of sand in the ocean, and the number of waves, and that we consider with amazement each drop of rain, each day and each hour of which the centuries are made, we are in raptures of admiration."[47]

*

The Fathers of the Desert not only loved God and neighbour; they practised true self-love.

A brother came to see Abba Agathon and said, "Allow me to live with you." However, on his way in, he had found a trinket on the road and he had brought it. "Where did you find that?" the old man asked. The brother replied, "On the road as I was walking." The old man said, "If you were coming to live with me, how did you pick up something you had not placed there yourself?" And he had him take the object back to where he had found it.[48]

102

Our conscience tells us what we must not do or what we must *leave out*. It will never tell us what *more* we should do. It does not have the power to do this. Our love of God alone has it. Natural conscience can make honest human beings of us, it will never make us saints. It seems to me that this is how we can interpret the words of St Paul: "I am not aware of anything against myself, but I am not thereby acquitted. It is the Lord who judges me" (1 Cor 4:4).

A sensitive conscience, among the Fathers of the Desert as among all the saints, has nothing to do with morbid scruples. It appears excessive only to those who do not know how a soul living in the divine presence can become more sensitive and refined.

Sometimes Abba Dioscorus would shed tears. His disciple would ask him, "Father, why are you crying?" "I am shedding tears over my sins", the old man would reply. The brother would then tell him, "Father, you have no sins." And the old man would say, "Truly, my child, if I were allowed to see my sins, three or four men would not be enough to shed tears over them."[49]

Cassian spoke about the fear of love: "This fear is not born from the dread of chastisement nor from the desire of a reward, but from the very greatness of love. It is an intermingling of the respect and attentive affection a son has for a father full of forbearance, a brother for his brother, a friend for his friend, a wife for her husband... what she fears is to hurt this love, to cause even the slightest hurt."[50]

This form of charity was also displayed in the desert, in the concern for authenticity: to be honest with oneself, with others, with God. Thought and word were never separated from the deed. To someone who was asking him how to behave with his disciples, Abba Poemen gave this advice: "Be a model for them; not someone who lays down laws." Here is another expression every bit as pithy:

"Let not your tongue do the speaking but your works."[51]

Teaching through example stood so much to reason with a certain abba that he never said anything to his disciple. The brother, surprised that he did not receive any orders from his elder, spoke of this to another old man. The latter came to see the abba and asked him the reason for his attitude. The abba told him, "I am not a superior who gives out orders; let him watch me live and let him do as I do."[52] Thought and word also had to go hand in hand. Abba Poemen said, "Teach your lips to say what is in your heart."[53]

*

Everything that has just been said on the charity of the Fathers of the Desert leads us to ask ourselves one question. There are certain improvements being made *among* humans as there are in the area of technology, and which can have moral repercussions. For instance, it is of no little importance that a physician called for an emergency should have a more rapid mode of transportation than in the past. But is there any improvement in the humans themselves? At a time rampant with violence and contempt of man, these examples may give us reason to doubt. There is, apparently, some progress with respect to a sense of awareness, but can we really speak of a progress if it has no influence on us at the practical level of life?

Be that as it may, the Fathers of the Desert show us that improvements in the human dimension are possible but that they are not linked to one specific era; it depends on the manner and the intensity with which divine filiation is lived. And they already denounced many illusions which were developed later.

At the beginning of this century, certain people elaborated on the idea that all evil comes from ignorance. There were then many illiterate people and one could think, indeed, that education, as it became generalized, would make people better. This idea has lost its credibility.

Then we greeted technology, with what enthusiasm! By improving living conditions, we thought we would, logically speaking, improve man and woman themselves. That idea also has lost its credibility!

Then there were – and still are – the astonishing discoveries of psychology by which it became possible to probe the depths of the human person. Some psychologists, who are unbelievers, think that basically the era of sin is over, as if it were linked with a pre-scientific period of humanity. There were no sinners, only sick people. From that moment, everything was simple: they would be cured and become good. There again, we have lost many of our illusions.

All this sounds very trivial today, that is true. We can however recall it to forestall other illusions of this nature which always lie in wait for us.

As far as the Fathers of the Desert are concerned, they had no illusions about this. They knew that there is no other solution to the fundamental human problem but to live the teaching of the Gospel, and that all other roads inevitably lead to a dead end. This is constantly proved by experience and the more we reject the Gospel message, the more we become entrenched in our own illusions.

If these men and women, often very crude to begin with, have become the personification of a charity expressed in delicate attentions which astonish us (let us but think of Abba Moses and his leaky jug), it is because they sought to live the Gospel message in its entirety as well as they could. In a word, they tried to become Christians. The message of the Fathers of the Desert, like that of the saints of all times, does not imply that the values of this world are to be rejected but that, in order to move toward a more human attitude, we must move toward holiness.

An apophthegm, better than lofty theories, reveals the

secret of this true charity. A brother had two tunics, a good one and a worthless one. A stranger came to beg from him. He gave the good one, kept the worthless one. Someone asked him, "Why did you not give the worthless one and keep the other which you wore at the assembly?" He replied, "Would you give the worthless one to Jesus?"[54] To see Christ in the brother is everything.

"The elders used to say that everyone must adopt the interests of his neighbour as his own so as to sustain him and in some way take him on to ourselves with his body and entirely bear the man... We must be compassionate in every way with him, they would say, rejoice and weep with him, in a word share his feelings as if we were the same body, as if we had the same face and the same soul. If he meets with some affliction, we must be as distressed as if that was happening to ourselves."[55]

But that charity, the very love of God poured into our hearts by the Holy Spirit, is it not vast to the point of overwhelming us? Isaac the Syrian wrote this magnificent text: "What is a charitable heart? It is a heart that enkindles itself with charity for the entire creation, for human beings, for birds, beasts, for devils, for all creatures. The one who has this heart will be unable to recall or see a creature without his eyes filling with tears because of the immense compassion which totally imbues his heart. He becomes gentle and cannot bear the sight or the knowledge of suffering of whatever nature, be it but a minor grief inflicted upon a creature... moved as he is by a pity which awakens in the heart of those who imbue themselves with the love of God."

*

So far we have observed the Fathers of the Desert practising charity among themselves, toward their neighbour other than monks without any exception, toward

God and, consequently, toward themselves. It would then seem that there is no more to say. This is not so at all. We have yet to examine an important aspect of their charity which has not even been mentioned. They benefited from the charity of others, in particular of Christian lay people, and there they drew upon one of the sources of their love for God and for humankind.

This charity could take on many forms. Sometimes, that of almsgiving as in this charming story. A poverty-stricken man came one day and knocked on the door of a hermit's lodging, but the latter had nothing to offer him as he was utterly destitute. So the poor man gave him the little he had.[56]

When Pachomius was still a pagan, he had been pressed to enlist in the Roman army. During the first stage of the convoy, some faithful gave food supplies and comforted the young recruits. Touched by this charity, Pachomius inquired about these people and learned that they were Christians. Then he cried out, "O God, if you help me escape the danger I am in, I too will serve men for the sake of your name."[57] This he did by organizing monastic life in community. Thus, at the origin of this movement destined to grow into such proportions in time and space, we find the charity of a few lay Christians. This example shows the incalculable and unforeseen repercussions of an act performed in the spirit of the Gospel.

Anthony was informed one day through a revelation that, through his charity and prayer, a physician of the city had reached the same degree of holiness as he had. And he even learned, always through revelation, that a cobbler of Alexandria had reached a higher degree of holiness than he had himself. He went to see him and questioned him. It was his humility and the awareness of his condition as a sinner before God that made him rise to such a high degree of holiness.[58]

Abba Macarius, on his part, finds out that he has not

reached the same degree of virtue as had two married women living in the city. He went to see them and they confided in him. They had promised the Lord never to let their thoughts wander, never to complain or lie, nor let themselves indulge in idle talk, and never to say disagreeable words to each other. And they had now been perfectly faithful to this vow for fifteen years.[59]

The very example of certain sinners could be of some benefit. Amma Sarah used to say, "My daily prayer is not that all believers be like me but that I be like them." A sister then told her, "Do you want to be like the sinners?" Sarah replied, "Certainly, I would like to have the zeal of those among them who continually say in a great spirit of hope, 'Let us do penance as soon as possible!'"

Here is a little-known apophthegm in which a lay person gives a monk a good lesson in discernment and wisdom. There was an abba of outstanding holiness, very devoted to God, famous for his arduous asceticism. One day, a man of high office in the empire came to see him with his retinue in order to hear a word of salvation from him. The abba, in keeping with his usual humility, began by telling him that he was not worthy of raising his eyes to heaven because of his hidden sins. "What is that compared to the sins we commit everyday, we the people of the world?" said the official. "No, no, I assure you," resumed the abba, "I am indeed the greatest sinner of all and I have but one thing in my head: I must have my place with those who do not deserve to see the face of the Lord, ending my life as I am doing, in neglect and unconcern."

While he was speaking in this way, some young men in the official's retinue were discussing among themselves. "Do you know what they are saying?" the official asked the abba. "No." "Well, this is what they are saying: 'We live in sin and we had the intention of converting ourselves. But really, if this monk, after a life of self-denial, has not only made no progress in virtue, but is still further away from God than at the beginning, it is not worth the effort. Let's keep on sinning!'" "That is not what I meant," the abba replied. "But that is what you said," retorted the official. "You see it is fine to be humble but we must be careful of what we say, we must take into account the circumstances and the people we are speaking to."[60]

The Fathers of these ancient times did not hesitate to suggest lay people as examples in all matters, including fasting, to the young brothers undergoing formation, as this apophthegm testifies. One day, an abba saw a burial procession go by. There was a large crowd following the hearse and among these people he saw two angels. Intrigued by their presence, he approached them and asked why they were there. They replied, "We are the angels of Wednesdays and Fridays. This person observed fasting faithfully on these days to the end. That is why we have come to the funeral, to honour this person."[61]

This charity in its many forms practised by people of the world of which the Fathers of the Desert now and then benefited so much is not necessarily ancient history. Monks may still receive lessons of this type. The Church is an assembly of brothers and sisters who, having diverse vocations, remain fragile human beings and need one another to make progress toward God.

NOTES

1. Pl. Deseille, *Les saint moines..., op. cit.*, p. 104.
2. J.-Cl. Guy, *op. cit.*, p. 396.
3. *Ibid.*, p. 325.
4. *Ibid.*, p. 96.
5. Abbot Isaïe, *op. cit.*, pp. 49-53.
6. *Ibid.*, pp. 56, 80.
7. J.-Cl. Guy, *op. cit.*, p. 183.
8. *Ibid.*, p. 67.
9. Abbot Isaïe, *op. cit.*, p. 281.

10. L. Regnault, II, *op. cit.*, p. 241.
11. J.-Cl. Guy, *op. cit.*, p. 391.
12. L. Regnault, *Série des anonymes, op. cit.*, p. 89.
13. *Ibid.*, p. 182.
14. *Ibid.*, p. 391.
15. *Ibid.*, p. 319.
16. *Ibid.*, p. 159.
17. L. Regnault, II, *op. cit.*, p. 223.
18. J.-Cl. Guy, *op. cit.*, p. 228.
19. *Ibid.*, p. 125.
20. *Ibid.*, p. 105.
21. *Ibid.*, p. 27.
22. L. Regnault, II, *op. cit.*, p. 74.
23. J.-Cl. Guy, *op. cit.*, p. 229.
24. *Ibid.*, p. 290.
25. *Ibid.*, p. 120.
26. *Ibid.*, p. 107.
27. L. Regnault, II, *op. cit.*, p. 103.
28. Pl. Deseille, *Guide spirituel, op. cit.*, p. 283. The purpose of this present work is not apologetic. However, we can quote a recent document from the Church's magisterium which amounts to a rehabilitation of the Fathers of the Desert and a justification for their contemplative life. After having recalled a famous word of ancient monasticism: "To be a monk is to have left everything and everyone in order to be united to everything and everyone", the document makes this comment on it: "He is united to everyone because he bears in his heart the adoration, the thanksgiving, the praise and the sufferings of the people of these times. He is united to everyone because God calls him to a place where he reveals his secret to creatures. They are present not only to the world, but also at the heart of the Church; such are the religious entirely devoted to contemplation." *Directoire sur la formation dans les Instituts religieux (Documentation catholique*, 15 April 1990).
29. Pl. Deseille, *Les saints moines..., op. cit.*, p. 128.
30. L. Regnault, III, *op. cit.*, p. 73.
31. J.-Cl. Guy, *op. cit.*, p. 50.
32. John Moschus, *op. cit.*, p. 103.
33. L. Regnault, III, *op. cit.*, p. 126.
34. J.-Cl. Guy, *op. cit.*, p. 88.
35. Abbot Isaïe, *op. cit.*, p. 289.
36. L. Regnault, *op. cit.*, p. 287.
37. J.-Cl. Guy, *op. cit.*, p. 48.
38. *Ibid.*, p. 262.
39. L. Regnault, *op. cit.*, p. 138.
40. J.-Cl. Guy, *op. cit.*, p. 132.
41. *Ibid.*, p. 32.
42. *Ibid.*, p. 295.
43. *Ibid.*, p. 45.
44. L. Regnault, *op. cit.*, p. 289.
45. J.-Cl. Guy, *op. cit.*, p. 134.

46. *Ibid.*, p. 249.
47. J. Cassian, *Conferences*, I, 15.
48. Abbot Isaïe, *op. cit.,* p. 286.
49. J.-Cl. Guy, *op. cit.*, p. 83.
50. J. Cassian, *Conferences*, XI, 13.
51. J.-Cl. Guy, *op. cit.*, p. 253.
52. *Ibid.*, p. 137.
53. *Ibid.*, p. 229.
54. L. Regnault, II, *op. cit.*, p. 284.
55. L. Regnault, *op. cit.*, p. 130.
56. John Moschus, *op. cit.*, p. 53.
57. Pl. Deseille, *op. cit.*, p. 52.
58. J.-Cl. Guy, *op. cit.*, p. 26.
59. L. Regnault, *op. cit.*, p. 170.
60. *Ibid.*, p. 162.
61. L. Regnault, III, *op. cit.*, p. 100.

6

A fruitful reading of Scripture

In the above pages, I often spoke of the biblical life of the Fathers of the Desert but I did so in a disconnected fashion. I thought it might be useful to treat this subject more systematically by devoting a chapter to it, however short it might be.

We have seen that their prayer was nourished by Scripture. According to the already quoted words of R. Draguet, "the Bible was the voice of their prayer." This was also true of their whole life of which we could say that it was steeped in the word of God.

The whole story of Anthony the Great is closely bound to Scripture. One day, while in church, he heard Jesus' words addressed to the rich young man, "If you wish to be perfect, go, sell your possessions, and give the money to the poor; then come, follow me" (Mt 19:21). He too was a rich young man; but contrary to the one of the Gospel, he immediately responded in a positive manner. This was the beginning of an extraordinary spiritual venture of which we know the outcome.[1]

His *Life*, written by St Athanasius, is interwoven with biblical quotations. "He was so attentive to its reading that nothing from Scripture escaped him," says his biographer, "and his memory took the place of books."[2]

He was to initiate a school of thought. Names of monks who, we are told, knew the whole Scripture by heart, are cited. In the Rule observed in Pachomian communities it is written, "There will be absolutely no one in the monastery who will not learn to read and who will not know parts of the Scriptures by heart, at least of the New Testament and the psalter."[3]

Speaking of the brothers of these same communities, an author of the time writes: "One ploughs the soil, another works in the garden, another is a blacksmith, another is in the bakery, in the carpenter's or in the fuller's workshops, another weaves large baskets, another is in the tannery, in the shoemaker's workshop or doing calligraphy, or again plaiting small baskets... And all of them recite the Scriptures from memory."[4]

*

But biblical science is no ordinary science; if one must make an effort to acquire it, the Holy Spirit also intervenes. He helps us to understand what he himself has inspired the sacred writers to write.

The famous Didymus the Blind offers us a proof of this. Effectively blind since the age of four, he received from the Spirit such a gift of knowledge in this domain that he made a complete commentary of the Old and the New Testament. His biographer tells us "that he scrutinized their teaching with such a keenness of mind and interpreted them so accurately and with such assurance that he outdid all the monks of ancient times."[5]

The virtue of humility is obviously required in order to receive the light of the Spirit. Many texts teach us that and ward off all presumption in this field.

A humility of this kind incites us to pray and ask for this light. Some brothers questioned Anthony about a verse in the *Book of Leviticus*. The old man withdrew into an isolated place and implored God saying, "O God, send Moses and he will explain this word to me."[6]

When Abba Pambo, who, nevertheless, was considered to be a great master, was questioned about a word of Scripture, he never replied immediately but he would say, "I have not found the answer yet." He often let three months go by before he gave an answer.[7]

One day, some brothers came to see Abba Anthony. Among them was Abba Joseph. In order to put them to the test, Anthony asked them to give their opinion on a scriptural text. Each one spoke in his turn, but Anthony would say, "You have not found the answer." Abba Joseph said, "As for me, I don't know." Then Anthony concluded, "Truly, Abba Joseph has found the way for he said, 'I do not know.'"[8]

To be humble in the understanding of Scripture also meant to be able to consult. An abba used to say, "The man who is doubtful about some point and does not go to be taught by those who know is like a dilapidated wall."[9]

An elder was said to have spent much time fasting in order to obtain from God the interpretation of a text in Scripture, and still he had no answer. He said to himself, "I took such pains for nothing... so I will go to my brother and question him." At that moment, an angel appeared to him and said, "Your fasts did not bring you any closer to God, but when you were humble enough to go to your brother, I was sent to give you the meaning of this text."[10]

Humility, obviously, does not exist without fraternal charity. Abba Isaïe wrote: "If there is discussion among you about a text of Scripture, let the one who knows and understands it yield his point of view as much as he can to that of his brother and bring peace to the latter in joy. The explanation sought is (essentially) this one: to humble oneself before one's brother."[11]

*

Knowing the Scriptures by heart is not enough. We could play on words and say that we must know it with the heart. According to a traditional and suggestive expression, it is advisable that one "ruminate" it incessantly. In this way, the spirit of the text conveyed by the letter penetrates the person and gradually transforms him or her.

We can imagine these monks filling their desert space with a noise sounding strange to us, a noise like the humming of thousands of insects. For these monks of ancient times were not familiar with our method of silent meditation; they would murmur what they were thinking. We already find evidence of that in Scripture: "The mouths of the righteous utter wisdom" (Ps 37:30).

An elder said, "The nature of water is to be soft, that of stone to be hard. But a jug hanging above a stone, allowing water to fall on it drop by drop, manages to pierce the stone. So it is for the Word of God; it is soft and our heart is hard. But the man who hears and meditates this Word opens his heart to the fear of God."[12]

The fear of love, of course, was defined by Cassian in the preceding chapter. Abba Isidore was said to have such an understanding of Scripture that sometimes he would forget about food and drink. His mind would take flight on this or that text of the sacred book, he would fall into ecstasy and tears flowed from his eyes.[13]

*

There was no doubt in the minds of the Fathers of the Desert about the importance of knowing the Bible. Among the counsels given by Anthony to someone who was asking him how to please God, we find this one: "Whatever you do, act according to the testimony of Holy Scripture."[14] To a brother who was constantly reading and meditating the sacred text, an abba would say, "You are going to the source of life."[15] Another used to say, "Not to know anything about the divine laws is a great betrayal of salvation." And again, "Ignorance of Scripture is a precipice and a deep chasm."[16]

What more precise advice do they give us on the importance of knowing the Scriptures for the growth of the life of union with God and for the struggle which this growth implies and demands?

St Paul in his *Letter to the Ephesians* compared the Word of God to the sword of the Spirit. In his counsels to Timothy he writes: "All scripture is inspired by God and is useful for teaching, for reproof, for correction, and for training in righteousness, so that everyone who belongs to God may be proficient, equipped for every good work" (2 Tim 3:16-17). If there is one teaching which was put into practice in the desert, this is the one.

Were they in need of spiritual help? The elders drew from the Bible as from an inexhaustible reservoir.

A brother was asking for advice about fighting against his passions which left him spent. The elder replied, "It is written, 'Call on me in the day of trouble; I will deliver you, and you shall glorify me' (Ps 50:15). So call on God and he will deliver you from all temptation."[17]

The Fathers used to say, "The monk must struggle all his life against acedia and discouragement. But", they would add, "he must not proudly take the credit for his victory for it is written: 'Unless the Lord builds the house, those who build it labour in vain' (Ps 127:1)." And in cases where those words of Scripture would be insufficient, he still would add two others (in this field, an abundance of resources does no harm!): 'For all human beings are dust and ashes' (Sir 17:32) and 'God opposes the proud, but gives grace to the humble' (Jas 4:6)."[18]

"Why is it that at certain times I am neglectful in matters pertaining to my soul?" a brother was asking. The elder replied, "Because you do not wish to fulfil what

117

Scripture says: 'I will bless the Lord at all times, his praise shall continually be in my mouth' (Ps 34:1). Wherever you go, wherever you are, you must constantly praise God, for divinity is not circumscribed in one place but is everywhere."[19]

A brother, who had fallen into a serious sin, came to see an abba who lacked discernment. The latter threw him into despair by telling him he had lost his soul. The brother then went to see Abba Sylvanius who demonstrated to him, using the Scriptures as a basis, that repentance and forgiveness were possible, and so his spirits were revived.[20]

Knowledge of the Bible could enable one to answer certain questions, not necessarily new ones, and restore inner peace. The superior of a community put the question: "Whose style of life is the better one, ours as we govern the brothers and lead them to salvation, or the style of those who struggle alone in the desert (the hermits)?" The answer was, "One must not take sides between Elijah and Moses, for both were pleasing to God."[21]

As could be expected, the sacred writ was used effectively against the devil.

"To meditate Scripture constantly," said Abba Isaïe, "is to leave no opening through which the enemy may enter into our hearts."[22] Another elder said, "A man terrifies the devils every time he reads the Holy Scriptures."[23]

Like Jesus tempted in the desert, Anthony triumphantly resisted the devil's assaults by using the Word of God. Verses spontaneously sprang from his lips.

"Do you wish to see Christ?" a devil asked a brother, undoubtedly wanting to make him fall into the dangerous pitfall of illusions. The brother replied, "I believe in my Christ who said, 'If anyone tells you: I am here, I am there, do not believe him.'" The defeated tempter immediately disappeared.[24]

"Do not contemn the psalms," says an abba, "for they

chase impure spirits from the soul and bring in the Holy Spirit." For anyone doubting this, the proof is given by Scripture: "Remember David who chanted the psalms with his zither and delivered Saul from the evil spirit."[25]

Finally, we are told that a brother was reciting from memory a text from the Holy Scriptures as he travelled down the road to the church.[26] A way as good as any to prepare oneself for the celebration of the Eucharist. Abba Isaïe would go so far as to say that the diligent meditation of Scripture was like a liturgical office which went on forever.[27]

We could speak of the thousand and one ways of using and living from Scripture.

*

To have a good knowledge of Scripture is a good thing provided it is put into practice.

"When you sit down to read the words of God," writes St John Chrysostom, "ask him first to open the eyes of your heart so that you may not only read them but also fulfil them, in such a way that we may not read through the lives and words of saints for our own condemnation."[28]

"We know the Scriptures by heart," an abba used to say; "we know all the psalms of David but we do not have what God is looking for: charity and humility." No doubt, this is an exaggeration which must precisely be ascribed to humility, but the lesson is always worth taking.[29]

Knowledge of the Scriptures enables one to make a good examination of conscience. A brother came to see an elder and asked him, "So, Abba, how are you?" The elder replied, "Poorly!" "Why?" Then came a long litany: "I am a liar and everyday I tell God: 'You condemn all those who lie.' I bear a grudge against my brother and I tell God: 'Forgive us as we forgive.' I put all my interest in food and I say: 'I have forgotten to eat my bread.' I sleep until morning and I chant: 'In the middle of the night, I rose to praise your name.' I who do not fast say: 'My knees are weak because of my fasts.' Whereas I am not ready, I say, 'My heart is ready, O God'."[30]

Some brothers went to Scete to see an elder. One of them said, "Abba, I have memorized the Old and the New Testament." The abba replied, "You have filled the air with words." The second one said, "As for me, I copied the Old and the New Testament in my own hand." The elder replied, "As for you, you have filled your closets with paper."[31]

A nun asked an abba, "I have learned the Old and the New Testament. What is there left for me to do?" The old man replied, "Is contempt for you the same as honour?" She said, "No." "Gain like loss, destitution like abundance?" She said, "No." The elder concluded, "You are deceiving yourself: you have not learnt the Old and the New Testament."[32]

Here is an apophthegm in contrast to this and giving an account of a deed both symbolic and charitable. A brother who had nothing else but a Gospel sold it to feed the poor. And he said, "I have sold the very words telling me: 'Sell all you have and give it to the poor'."[33]

*

While acknowledging the importance of the sacred book, the Fathers of the Desert did not scorn the commentaries which can help to have a better understanding of its meaning.

Moreover, they knew that the meditation of Scripture is only a means among others to accede to the perfection of charity.

A brother questioned Abba Poemen and said, "I want to learn the Scriptures a little." The old man said, "Surely, that is advisable for you." The brother resumed, "Learning many texts from the Scriptures will interrupt my manual work." And Abba Poemen replied, "Work is also a teaching and a lesson."[34]

An elder said, "The one sitting in his cell and meditating Scripture is like a man who is looking for the king. But the one who prays constantly is like the man who speaks to the king. As for the one who implores with tears, he clasps the feet of the king and begs for his pity, as did the courtesan who, in a short time, had washed all her sins away with her tears."[35]

We also find warnings against a false interpretation of Scripture. History shows that the Bible can be used to justify anything and that has been done, alas, to justify, for instance, slavery, racism, abuse of conscience... Sometimes using a verse out of context is enough and that is still evident today.[36] It does not surprise us to learn from the Fathers of the Desert that the devil makes a powerful contribution to this falsification of the sacred text and, obviously, the ally in his territory is pride.

We are told that a certain Abba Hero justified his proud independent attitude with these words of Christ: "Call no one on earth 'Master'". His mind completely gave way, then he fell into religious indifference. But after a serious illness, a few days before he died, thanks to God, he repented.[37]

One day, a devil came before an abba who had his son with him and he persuaded him to re-enact the sacrifice of Abraham. Fortunately, when the child saw his father sharpening his knife and looking for ropes to bind him up, he guessed the crime his father was about to commit and he fled terrified.[38]

*

We have seen the monks of the desert interpreting Scripture in a way that is familiar to us. However, this was not their only way of deriving benefit from the word of God. They knew another method which is baffling to us. It can be described as *accommodating*. That is, it consists in "accommodating" the sacred text to the goal pursued. Some examples will make us understand that better and will show the interest in doing things this way in order to advance in spiritual life.

It is said in Scripture that Noah, Job and Daniel were pleasing to God. Abba Poemen drew the following conclusion: "Noah represents poverty, Job, affliction, and Daniel, discernment. Hence, if these three works are found in man, the Lord dwells in him."[39]

The same abba again says, "When he was a shepherd and fighting against a lion, David grasped its throat and killed it instantly. If, therefore, we also take hold of our own throat and of our belly (an allusion to gluttony) we will, thanks to God, triumph over the invisible lion."[40]

An elder remembered that Joseph of Arimathea had wrapped Jesus' body in a clean linen cloth and laid it in a new tomb. He sees there an image of the renewed man we must try to become, in whom Christ comes to dwell.[41]

Someone questioned Abba Sisoës, "What do the psalms say about idols?" The old man replied, "They have mouths and do not speak, they have eyes and do not see, they have ears and do not hear." A good opportunity for the abba to recall the importance of being recollected: "So must the monk be", he concluded.[42]

Some ancient legal texts of the Old Testament, which lay down rules about food and are completely out-of-date as far as we are concerned, were still a source of life for the Fathers of the Desert. One of them used to say, "The pure animal has a divided hoof and chews its cud or ruminates its food. Therefore, we, who have really believed and accepted the two Testaments, must ruminate the good and not the bad reading. Now, the beneficial food is the good thoughts given to us by the tradition of holy masters and the reading of Scripture: the one who loves God must always meditate these. As for the bad food, it is the impure thoughts inspired by the devils. We must reject them as soon as they suggest themselves and we must not dwell on them."[43]

Similarly, the historical narratives of the people of the Old Testament were meditated and people knew how to draw a timely teaching from what, for us, constitutes ancient history and no more.

Thus it was that the main vices, indexed and analyzed by Cassian, corresponded to the nations occupying the Promised Land and had to be exterminated. One difficulty, however, faced our author: the vices were eight in number and the nations concerned were but seven. The problem was quickly resolved. The eighth vice was gluttony. "Taking food is an innate, natural inclination for us and it is almost impossible to get rid of the cupidity and the superfluous desires in this domain." It is then related to the Egyptians whom the Hebrews did not exterminate but always kept at a distance. We do the same by rejecting all thoughts of dishes that are too dainty and in being satisfied with simple and frugal food.[44]

In the year 587 before Christ, Nebuzaradan, chief of the guards of Nebuchadnezzar, king of Babylon, took Jerusalem and deported almost the whole population. This military leader was identified with the chief cook of the palace. A good opportunity for our biblists of the desert. A brother questioned an elder, "What does the desire to eat and drink without discretion create in man?" The elder replied, "It gives rise to every form of evil. Indeed, we see that the final destruction of Jerusalem was brought about by the cook Nebuzaradan. In his turn, the Lord advised his disciples: 'Watch that your hearts may not become heavy with loose living, drunkenness and the anxieties of life.'"[45]

Our biblists did not give us only a few short maxims. Abba Isaïe commented entire passages of the Bible in this way.

Do you know, for instance, why Rebecca sent her son Jacob in Mesopotamia? The sacred text tells us: "To make him escape the vengeance of his brother Esau from whom he had taken away the blessing of the birthright, and to find a wife (in fact, he was to take two wives: Leah and Rachel)."[46] But our author discovers another hidden reason which undoubtedly would not have come to our minds. "Mesopotamia is called thus because it is situated between two rivers, the Tigris and the Euphrates. Tigris means 'discernment' and Euphrates, 'humility'." Jacob, in fact, would need these two virtues.

As far as his wives are concerned, they too are symbolic. It is written that Jacob loved Rachel more than Leah. Leah, whom he married first, had poor eyesight. This means that as long as one is in physical labour (the ascetic life of the beginner), one does not yet see the glory of true contemplation. But to wed Rachel, she being absolutely perfect, is to become a contemplative. We could go on and on.[47]

*

This manner of interpreting Scripture, which I have described as "accommodating" and which bears various names among the experts, was also that of the Fathers of the Church. St Paul had already used it in his letters. Alluding to an episode in the life of the Hebrews in the desert, he writes, "They drank from the spiritual rock that followed them, and the rock was Christ" (1 Cor 10:4). In order to prove that to be an unbeliever is inexcusable since the faith has been proclaimed everywhere, in his *Letter to the Romans* he quotes Psalm 18: "Their voice has gone out to all the earth, and their words to the ends of the world" (Rom 10:18).

Indeed, the fact that the heavens proclaim the glory of God is mentioned in this psalm. The bond between the psalmist contemplating the firmament and drawing from it his praise to God as creator and the preachers proclaiming the salvation of the world is rather loose!

Actually, the association of ideas and images are not so naive and are far from being fruitless. Another text of Scripture could be recalled, that is, the news formerly told to Abraham, the Father of the believers, and contribute to nourish the faith of Paul's correspondents: "Look toward heaven and count the stars, if you are able to count them: so shall your descendants be" (Gen 15:5).

Without going so far as to adopt this method of exegesis practised in its pure and simple form by the Fathers of the Desert, may we not conclude from this that we have something to learn from them in this field so that we may soft-pedal our excessively rigorous logic, often dried up and having a drying effect, in order to live and communicate our faith more effectively?

*

We know of no better way of summing up the biblical life of the Fathers of the Desert than by quoting the text of St Augustine: "Yesterday, you understood a little; today, you understand better; tomorrow, you will understand better still: the light of God is growing in you."

NOTES

1. St Athanasius, *op. cit.*, p. 124.
2. *Ibid.*, p. 25.
3. Pl. Deseille, *Les saint moines...*, *op. cit.*, p. 55.
4. Palladius, *op. cit.*, p. 98.
5. *Ibid.*, p. 45.
6. J.-Cl. Guy, *op. cit.*, p. 26.

7. Palladius, *op. cit.*, p. 54.
8. J.-Cl. Guy, *op. cit.*, p. 23.
9. L. Regnault, *op. cit.*, II, p. 262.
10. L. Regnault, *Série des anonymes, op. cit.,* p. 109.
11. Abbot Isaïe, *op. cit.*, p. 79.
12. J.-Cl. Guy, *op. cit.*, p. 256.
13. Palladius, *op. cit.*, p. 41.
14. J.-Cl. Guy, *op. cit.*, p. 20.
15. L. Regnault, *op. cit.*, II, p. 290.
16. J.-Cl. Guy, *op. cit.*, p. 87.
17. L. Regnault, *op. cit.*, II, p. 20.
18. *Ibid.*, p. 45.
19. *Ibid.*, p. 55.
20. L. Regnault, *op. cit.*, p. 84.
21. L. Regnault, *op. cit.*, II, p. 39.
22. Abbot Isaïe, *op. cit.*, p. 251.
23. L. Regnault, *op. cit.*, II, p. 220.
24. L. Regnault, *op. cit.*, p. 109.
25. L. Regnault, *op. cit.*, III, p. 86.
26. L. Regnault, *op. cit.*, p. 207.
27. Abbot Isaïe, *op. cit.*, p. 251.
28. L. Regnault, *Série des anonymes*, op. cit., p. 293.
29. *Ibid.*, p. 85.
30. L. Regnault, *op. cit.*, II, p. 112.
31. L. Regnault, *op. cit.*, p. 129.
32. *Ibid.*, p. 189.
33. *Ibid.*, p. 130.
34. L. Regnault, *op. cit.*, II, p. 287.
35. *Ibid.*, p. 107.
36. We know that *apartheid* is a political doctrine developed from a certain reading of the Bible.
37. Palladius, *op. cit.*, p. 89.
38. J. Cassian, *Conferences*, II, 7, *op. cit.*
39. J.-Cl. Guy, *op. cit.*, p. 229.
40. *Ibid.*, p. 254.
41. L. Regnault, *op. cit.*, II, p. 20.
42. L. Regnault, *op. cit.*, p. 129.
43. *Ibid.*, p. 289.
44. J. Cassian, *Conferences*, V, 17-19, *op. cit.*
45. L. Regnault, *op. cit.*, II, p. 73.
46. Cf Genesis chapter 27.
47. Abbot Isaïe, *op. cit.*, pp. 69-70.

7

An innate optimism

In the behaviour of the men and women of the desert there is this deep underlying idea: sin has instigated in and around us a kind of more or less generalized anarchy and it is a matter of restoring order by struggling against evil. This also means restoring peace in ourselves, in our relationships with God and others, with the entire creation. They would have said: restoring a harmony such as existed for Adam and Eve before the fall. That is indeed an essential theme of their spirituality.

The Fathers of the Desert well knew that Jesus Christ had done more than repair a broken world, that he had brought it to its fulfilment with his new creation in the Spirit. Besides, the fact that they interpreted the first chapters of the *Book of Genesis* in a historically simplistic manner matters little. For lack of a tangible experience of this new world which is the domain of faith, they went to find, as it were, a reflection of the Paradise where this universal harmony reigned before sin. They saw there, so to speak, the symbol of the hope by which they lived and which, they knew, would not deceive them.

In the account of *Genesis*, it is also said that God created humankind in his own image (cf Gen 1:27). But sin distorts this resemblance and we become caricatures of the image of God.

If the Fathers of the Desert launched themselves into the spiritual battle, it was to arrive at a purity of heart that would allow this work to be integrally restored: to restore harmony in creation and become again an image of God. With the certitude of faith that never left them, this was not only possible but already mysteriously on the way to full realization.

*

This certitude of faith is revealed by an important theme in the ancient monastic literature which, at first glance, may be astonishing: the relationship with untamed animals.

In the figurative account of the origins, the man assigns a name to all the animals, including the wild beasts. To give a name, according to biblical mentality, is to take possession of what one names, to bind it to one's person, to one's service. Man was enthroned in the work of God, destined to preside over the universal harmony destroyed by sin (cf Gen 2:19-20).

In striking contrast with life in Paradise, these animals became hostile to man as a result of sin. Very often, the psalmist cannot find more powerful images to evoke those who have designs against his life. In the books of *Daniel* and *Revelation*, they symbolize the bestiality, the brutality of the great empires which aspire to world domination, enemies of Christ and the saints, spreading death and ruin in their path. One of them has enormous teeth of iron; it devours and tramples over whatever it cannot eat. They have strange shapes, as if the inspired authors thereby wanted to show that sin distorts creation.

In the literature of the Fathers of the Desert, the idea that a restored friendship with God re-establishes harmony in our situation is constantly emphasized. There are many texts on this subject. First, Anthony the Great may be quoted as a typical example. "And it was an astonishing fact", writes his biographer, "that alone in the desert, in the presence of so many wild beasts, he was not afraid of their ferocious nature; wild beasts lived at peace with him."[1]

Since visitors were attracted by his holiness and were coming to him in increasing numbers he decided to grow some vegetables to feed them. At first, when the wild beasts of the desert came to drink, they often damaged his seed beds and his crops. He told them, "Why do you do me harm while I do no harm to any of you? In the name of the Lord, do not come here anymore."[2] The wild beasts abided by what he had forbidden them to do. One is reminded of Francis of Assisi.

Sometimes, man and beast lived together and even shared the same food. We are told that Abba Agathon came to live in a grotto in the desert. It was already sheltering a large serpent. The latter, politely, wanted to leave and let the abba have the space. Abba Agathon did not let himself be outdone in amiability: "If you go, I won't settle here", he said. And the serpent stayed. They fed together on a sycamore in the neighbourhood.[3]

In other accounts, lions do more than peacefully live with the Fathers of the Desert; they simply and absolutely wait on them. They are seen helping with the water chore or leading the donkey to pasture...

In the life of Paul of Thebes, we are told that two lions came to dig out the grave of this holy man, who is considered to be the first Christian hermit. Anthony was present and, once the work was completed, the grave diggers for the occasion asked for his blessing.[4]

The doctrine of this astonishing solidarity was explained by an author of the sixth century, a biographer of the Fathers of the Desert. Speaking of one of them, he wrote: "Besides the other graces he possessed, he had also received from God the gift of suffering no harm from the carnivorous and venomous beasts with which he constantly lived." And he concludes, "When God dwells in a man and takes his rest there, all beings are subjected to him as they were to Adam before he transgressed God's commandment."[5]

But we must also quote an apophthegm which, on the whole, acts as a counter-proof to this spirituality always naively expressed in figurative language. A lion had entered into the service of a hermit. Everyday he led the donkey to pasture. It so happened that the disciple of this hermit fell into sin. The lion immediately became wild and broke the donkey's neck.

*

One must note that this symbolic and fundamental theme of the peaceful cohabitation of men and beasts has its source in Scripture where the nostalgia for the lost Paradise persists and shows up here and there. In an idealistic prophetic text familiar to us, since it appears in the Advent liturgy, Isaiah sketches the picture of the restored paradisiaic life when the kingdom of the King-Messiah will come: "The wolf shall live with the lamb, the leopard shall lie down with the kid, the calf and the lion and the fatling together, and a little child shall lead them... The nursing child shall play over the hole of the asp, and the weaned child shall put its hand on the adder's den. They will not hurt or destroy in all my holy mountain" (Is 11:6-9).

In the *Book of Hosea* this same theme is related to the restored fidelity: "For I will remove the names of the Baals from her mouth, and they shall be mentioned by name no more. I will make for you a covenant on that day with the wild animals, the birds of the air, and the creeping things of the ground" (Hos 2:17-18). In *Ezekiel*, it is written: "I will make with them a covenant of peace and banish wild animals from the land" (Ezek 34:25). And in the *Book of Job*, it is said: "... you shall not fear the wild animals of the earth" (Job 5:22).

We may also quote texts where we see beasts, who normally escape from the control of the man, enter into the service of the friends of God. So it was for Elijah: "The word of the Lord came to him, saying, 'Go from here and turn eastward, and hide yourself by the Wadi Cherith, which is east of the Jordan. You shall drink from the wadi, and I have commanded the ravens to feed you there... The ravens brought him bread and meat in the morning, and bread and meat in the evening; and he drank from the wadi" (1 Kings 17:2-4,6).

In the short account of Jesus' temptation in the desert, Mark tells us that "he was with the wild beasts" (Mk 1:12-13), and this text should probably be interpreted in this same spirit. Moreover, at the end of the Gospel, Mark says that those who have believed "will pick up snakes in their hands" and they will not be hurt. A prophecy which comes true for St Paul on the island of Malta. After the shipwreck, the natives "kindle a fire" and, as he throws a bundle of brushwood on the fire, Paul is bitten by a viper. He suffers no harm, to the great astonishment of the inhabitants of the island who conclude he is a god (cf Acts 28:1- 6).

The same St Paul writes: "For the creation waits with eager longing for the revealing of the children of God; for the creation was subjected to futility, not of its own will but by the will of the one who subjected it, in hope that the creation itself will be set free from its bondage to decay and will obtain the freedom of the glory of the children of God. We know that the whole creation has been groaning in labour pains until now" (Rom 8:19-22).

Was Paul thinking of animals when he wrote that? The theme cherished by the Fathers of the Desert, which I have just pointed out, calls for a comment. How could we think that our inferior brothers, the animals, among which many have been the servants of man and woman, for instance, the dog leading the blind or being devoted to the point of giving up its life for its master; or again the cat, the pet animal of the elderly living alone, which has prevented the latter from sinking into despair; how could we think, therefore, that these companions of our life here below would be excluded from this transformation and glorification of the cosmos, even if the modes of their future existence still remain a mystery?

*

From this eminently Christian vision of the world, the Fathers of the Desert have drawn a fundamental optimism which is revealed mainly in their attitude in face of death, in their contentions with the devils and in their unshakable faith in divine mercy.

First, their attitude in face of death. What is striking in these old texts is the importance given to the remembrance of the dead.

"If there are graves in the area where you live, go to them constantly," advises an elder, "and meditate on those lying there... And when you hear that a brother is about to leave this world to go to the Lord, go and stay with him in order to contemplate on how a soul leaves the body."[6]

"A truly philosophical work", says an abba to philosophers visiting him, "is to meditate constantly on death."[7]

We are told that a certain elder practised the following. Always seated in his cell, serious and bent over toward the ground, he would say while groaning, "What will happen to me?" Then, keeping silent for about an hour, he would work. Then, again, he would groan and say, "What will happen to me?" Thus he would spend all his days, meditating on his soul leaving his body.[8]

Evidently, our sensitivity is altogether different and it would seem that speaking here about optimism would be exaggerated; that is the least we could say. However, texts of this type must not be separated from a rather large number of accounts of the deaths of the Fathers in the desert. And there, we can truly speak of optimism. The very embellishments we find there are often significant: they show that they did not undergo the pain of leaving this world but experienced their death as a celebration.

Anthony's face was radiant with joy as he died. All those who were witnesses to the death of Pachomius saw a multitude of angels preceding him, singing with great joy.[9]

As for Abba Sisoës, his "birth in heaven" – according to the beautiful traditional expression of the Church – is described in an account that deserves to be quoted in full. While the Fathers were sitting around him, his face shone like the sun. He said to them, "Here comes Abba Anthony." A little later, he said, "Here comes the choir of prophets." And the radiance of his face doubled in intensity; and here he was speaking, as it were, with someone. The elders asked him, "Who are you speaking with, Father?" He replied, "The angels are coming to fetch me and I am begging them to let me do more penance." The elders said, "You do not need to do penance, Father." But Abba Sisoës insisted, "In truth, I am not even aware that I am still but beginning." And they all knew that he was perfect. And again his face suddenly became like the sun and they were all filled with awe. He said to them, "Look, the Lord is coming and he says, 'Bring me the vase of the desert.'" And there was, as it were, a lightning flash and the whole house was filled with fragrance.[10]

Other accounts, more restrained in tone, are almost sublime in their simplicity.

Two elders were walking in the desert. They heard the feeble sound of a voice rising from the earth. They looked for the entrance to the cave and, there, they discovered a nun, reclined and ill. They asked her, "When did you come here, Amma? Who is taking care of you?" "I have spent thirty-eight years in this grotto, serving Christ and never lacking anything," she replied, "and until today, I saw no one. God has sent you to bury my body." With these words she fell into the sleep of the Lord. The abbas praised God and went back to their home after they had buried the body.[11]

Abba Moses questioned Brother Zachary who was at the point of death, "What do you see?" he asked him. "Father, would it not be preferable to keep silent?" "That is true, my child, be silent," Moses answered. And at that moment of his death, Abba Isidore, who was present, raised his eyes to heaven and said, "Rejoice, my child Zachary, the gates of the kingdom of heaven are open for you."[12]

Death could be more tragic but it was, nevertheless, a moment of celebration. Such was that of Moses (the ex-brigand). The brothers said to him, "Let us flee, the Barbarians are coming. And you, Father, flee as well." "Oh me," he replied, "I have been waiting so long for this day so that the word of my Lord Jesus Christ may be fulfilled: 'All those who have used the sword will die by the sword.'" There were seven brothers with him. Suddenly, they said, "The Barbarians are here at the door!" They erupted into the hut and massacred everyone there. One of the brothers ran out to hide under cords of palm trees. There he saw seven crowns coming down to rest on the heads of Abba Moses and his six brothers killed with him.[13]

It is true that, in the apophthegms, one finds echoes of fear when facing the prospect of death. It is, one could say, normal and natural; we are facing the unknown, confronting an unfathomable mystery. The Christian, moreover, believes in a judgement and knows that he or she is a sinner.

Abba Agathon (whose tactful charity is still remembered) kept his eyes open, motionless, at the time of his death. The brothers shook him saying, "Where are you?" He replied, "Before God's tribunal." They retorted, "Father, are you afraid too?" "Up until now," he said, "I have kept the commandments as best I could; but I am a man, how can I know if my work is pleasing to God?" Nevertheless, he died in joy, and to his brothers he gave the impression that he was greeting friends.[14]

The "great passage" (death) is seen by the Fathers of the Desert with a spirit of faith which St Benedict, their spiritual heir, echoes in his Rule when he says that one must "constantly have death before one's eyes."[15] This is not meant to be a morbid attitude and it could be translated as follows and still be true to its meaning: Keep your eyes constantly fixed on the door about to be opened, as when we are waiting for a person dear to us. We often look at this door about to open to let that person in. And as soon as that person is there – we have all had this experience – our life is suddenly transformed; this is the image of Christian death.

A door wide open... when "our sister death" arrives, as St Francis of Assisi used to say.

For the Fathers of the Desert, death evokes the exact opposite of a "dark hole": it is an unlimited space filled with light. Without any doubt, they would have loved the famous angel of the cathedral of Rheims with his enigmatic smile and acting as the gatekeeper of future life; there is the enigma, there is also the smile... And even laughter! We are told, in an apophthegm, that an abba died while laughing, making fun in a nice way of those still remaining on earth, the place of labour, while he was passing on to that of rest.[16]

*

This optimism is also revealed in the Fathers of the Desert in their contentions with the devil. The devil and his angels are very much a part of their universe. They eventually even see them with their eyes of flesh. The devil is the most powerful enemy there is and yet they are not afraid, for they know that his defeat is certain, even if he is still malignant for a while. They fight against him, certain that they can rely on the strength from above.

"The devil was caught on a baited hook", Anthony used to tell his disciples. "When the Lord came the enemy was crushed and his forces were broken down. So, being helpless, he is like a tyrant who, having lost all his power, cannot meanwhile remain at rest."[17]

Again he used to say, "The devils do not have any power even over pigs. It is written in the Gospel that they prayed the Lord in this way: 'Allow us to go into those pigs'. If they have no power even over pigs, all the more reason not to have any on man made in the image of God."[18]

The mere sight of a habit which had belonged to a famous abba was enough to put the devil to flight. Or a simple sign of the cross: "Make the sign of the cross on yourself," Anthony would tell his visitors frightened by the manifestations of the enemy, "and go, do not let them dampen your spirits." The visitors would leave, using the symbol of the presence of Christ as protection.[19]

Besides, the snares of the devil can be turned against himself, for there is a positive side to temptation. An abba went so far as to affirm, "Do away with temptation and no one will be saved."[20] Another explains this maxim in this way: "If the tree is not shaken by the wind, it does not take root and does not grow. So is the monk: if he is not tempted and does not bear with temptation, he does not become strong."[21] Did not the devil teach them to pray by setting traps which forced them to cry out to God? And the cry is the most beautiful of prayers.

Other texts, however, show us that optimism in the desert was not smug but realistic. The victory of Christ over "the Prince of this world", as St John calls him, is an established fact. Evil forces cannot have the last word. But as long as we are here below, we must fight and partial defeats are still possible.

An abba said, "Don't rely on yourself, my brother, until you have left your body, for if you say that you are dead (to temptation), Satan is still there to tempt you."[22] A recommendation well illustrated in an apophthegm where we see a devil appear to a monk at the point of death. The devil tells him, "You have defeated me." The dying man offers a prudent answer, "I do not know yet."[23]

The Fathers of the Desert, like all of us, were confronted with the reality of sin, and sin, this accomplice of the enemy, appears in many forms. When we run through the ancient monastic writings, we cannot help but see the importance of the struggle they led on a particular front: the fear of being unfaithful to their celibacy. How many times do we not see them in the throes of this temptation? They do not always come out victorious! Their image of women, we must admit, is more often that of the temptress.

In fact, as a more attentive reading shows, their reactions to having committed this sin proves that it was not of prime importance to them. The most terrifying danger was not there. A view of things, more evangelical than the one we will have later at certain periods of history, made them see that the number one enemy of the Christians, Satan's most terrible ally, is pride. Consequently, to fight it, they used the most effective weapon there is: humility.

Someone asked Abba Longinus, "Which is the greatest of all virtues?" The elder replied, "Since pride is the father of all vices, since it brought about the downfall of certain ones in heaven, I think humility is the greatest of virtues, for it makes man climb again out of abysses, even if the sinner is like a demon."[24]

Abba Anthony said, "I saw all the snares of the enemy

spread over the earth and I said with a groan, 'Who will go past these snares?' And I heard a voice answering me: Humility.'"[25]

If we believe Amma Theodora, the devils themselves admitted they were helpless in face of this formidable weapon. She would say, indeed, that neither asceticism nor any other suffering can save, but only true humility. Then she would cite the case of a hermit who would drive away evil spirits and ask them, "What makes you leave? Is it our fasting?" They would answer, "We neither eat nor drink." "Is it the vigils?" They would answer, "We do not sleep." "Is it being away from the world?" "We live in deserts." "By what power do you then leave?" They would reply, "Nothing can triumph over us except humility."[26]

To theoretical teaching, concrete examples would be added.

Someone possessed by the devil struck a monk on the cheek. The abba immediately presented the other cheek. The devil fled, defeated by this humility.[27]

In another case of demonic possession, an abba ordered the evil spirit, "Come out of this creature of God!" The devil replied, "First, I want to ask you one question. Tell me, which ones are the goat and which ones are the sheep?" The elder answered, "I am the goat; as for the sheep, God knows them." At these words the devil came out of the possessed man.[28]

Certain snares of the enemy were laid out in a more subtle way; they were no less outwitted. The devil, disguised as an "angel of light", appeared to one of the brothers and said, "I am Gabriel, and I was sent to you." The brother replied, "See if you have not been sent to someone else. As for me, I am not worthy of such an honour." The devil immediately disappeared.[29]

An elder summed up this combat with one of these well-coined expressions of which the Fathers of the Desert had the secret: "The one who possesses humility humiliates the devils; the one who is not humble is humiliated by them."[30]

*

Finally, another aspect of the optimism of the Fathers of the Desert who knew they were sinners and, therefore, able to fall into sin, even serious ones, was to believe in the power of divine mercy. The devil also knew that God is merciful. That is why, when these men fell into sin, the devils would try to drive them to despair.

A brother, who was fetching some water, met a laundrywoman and sinned with her. The devils then troubled his soul by suggesting these thoughts to him, "Where do you think you will go now? There is no salvation for you." The brother, who understood their manoeuvres, replied incessantly, "I have not sinned, I have not sinned!" An elder, who was informed of the affair, congratulated him, "Through your discernment, you have triumphed over the power of the enemy."[31]

This brother had sinned, to be sure! But Christ has triumphed over sin, and with sin he has triumphed over the sinner's despair. Judas could have become a great saint if he had known that. For his greatest sin was not his betrayal but his lack of trust in the possibility of being forgiven. It is because he trusted the Lord that Simon Peter became a saint in spite of his three denials.

A monk was the friend of a hermit. When this hermit died, the monk found some gold coins in his hermitage. He began to cry for fear that his friend would be rejected by God because of this money. As he was praying very much for him, an angel appeared to him and said, "Why are you so anxious? If everybody were perfect, how could divine mercy manifest itself?"[32]

In the desert, as in all milieux of life, fraternal correction possibly had to be practised. Their manner of speak-

139

ing about that gives us a good idea of the conception these old monks had of divine benevolence.

"Brother," said an elder, "if you must reprimand someone, here is a commandment: May mercy always outweigh everything in your scale... You will feel within yourself the mercy God has for the world."[33]

Some questioned Abba Sisoës, "If a brother sins, doesn't he need to do penance for a year?" He replied, "Those are harsh words." The visitors resumed, "For six months?" He answered, "That is much." They said, "For forty days?" Again he said, "That is much." They said to him, "So how much? If a brother falls into sin and it happens that we immediately have the agape, will he be a part of this fraternal celebration as well?" The elder told them, "No, but he needs to do penance for a few days. For I trust that if such a man does penance with all his heart, even in three days, God will receive him."[34] Could we not say that it is God himself who is speaking?

We are more demanding for others as a rule than God is. Sometimes it is also for ourselves that we lack mercy more than he does. And yet, the Holy Spirit has said through the voice of the prophet Isaiah, "Though your sins are like scarlet, they shall be like snow; though they are red like crimson, they shall become like wool" (Is 1:18). He also says in the *First Letter of John*, "Whenever our hearts condemn us, God is greater than our hearts" (1 Jn 3:20).

One day when his past was coming up in his mind to the point of giving him nausea, Abba Moses, his courage having vanished, took refuge with Abba Isidore. Then Abba Isidore led him outside and, pointing toward the west, showed him devils armed for war. Then he made him look to the east. There he saw a multitude of angels in glory, infinitely more numerous. The west, where the sun sets, symbolizes the end of day. The east symbolizes a new dawn, a new sun, a new light, a new day.[35]

The man of the desert knows he is saved, incorporated as he is into Christ's victory by divine mercy: this is evoked so effectively in the figurative style of this text. The Most High has done marvels for him and in him. He can sing his own *Magnificat*, and that is how we can describe the following apophthegm:

Someone told Abba John the Persian, "We have borne great afflictions because of the kingdom of heaven: will we inherit it?" The abba said, "As for me, I trust I will inherit the Jerusalem from above. And why should I not trust it will be so? I have become hospitable like Abraham, meek like Moses, holy like Aaron, patient like Job, humble like David, a hermit like John, filled with compunction like Jeremiah, a master like Paul, a believer like Peter, wise like Solomon. And like the good thief, I have full confidence: The one who out of his goodness has given me so much will also give me the Kingdom."[36]

NOTES

1. St Athanasius, *op. cit.*, p. 63.
2. *Ibid.*, p. 62.
3. L. Regnault, II, *op. cit.*, p. 278.
4. R. Draguet, *op. cit.*, p. 85.
5. Cyril of Scythopolis, in *Les Moines d'Orient*, III, Paris, 1962, p. 77.
6. L. Regnault, *Série des anonymes*, op. cit., p. 227.
7. *Ibid.*, p. 303.
8. *Ibid.*, p. 196.
9. R. Draguet, *op. cit.*, pp. 72 and 121.
10. J.-Cl. Guy, *op. cit.*, p. 279.
11. L. Regnault, *Série des anonymes*, *op. cit.*, p. 52.
12. J.-Cl. Guy, *op. cit.*, p. 99.
13. *Ibid.*, p. 185.
14. Abbot Isaïe, *op. cit.*, p. 287.
15. Règle des moines, chapter 4.
16. J.-Cl. Guy, *op. cit.*, p. 373.
17. St Athanasius, *op. cit.*, p. 45.
18. *Ibid.*, p. 47.
19. *Ibid.*, p. 33.
20. L. Regnault, II, *op. cit.*, p. 130.

21. L. Regnault, *Série des anonymes, op. cit.*, pp. 131 and 231.
22. J.-Cl. Guy, *op. cit.*, p. 370.
23. L. Regnault, II, *op. cit.*, p. 99.
24. *Ibid.*, p. 104.
25. J.-Cl. Guy, *op. cit.*, p. 21.
26. *Ibid.*, p. 118.
27. L. Regnault, *Série des anonymes, op. cit.*, p. 106.
28. *Ibid.*, p. 118 (an allusion to Mt 25).
29. *Ibid.*, p. 109.
30. *Ibid.*, p. 182.
31. *Ibid.*, p. 31.
32. L. Regnault, II, *op. cit.*, p. 40.
33. Pl. Deseille, *Guide spirituel, op. cit.*, p. 134.
34. J.-Cl. Guy, *op. cit.*, p. 281.
35. J.-Cl. Guy, *op. cit.*, p. 183.
36. *Ibid.*, p. 149.

Bibliography

P.F. Anson, *Partir au désert. Vingt siècles d'érémitisme*, Paris, 1967.

St Athanasius, *Life of Antony and Letter to Marcellinus*, SPCK, 1980.

PL. Deseille, *Les saints moines d'Orient: Textes choisis*, Namur, 1958.

PL. Deseille, "Guide spirituel" in *Collectanea Cisterciensia*, 1969.

R. Draguet, *Les Pères du désert: Textes choisis*, Paris, 1949.

John Cassian, *Conférences*, I-VII, by E. Pichery, Cerf (SC), Paris, 1955.

John Cassian, *Conférences*, VIII-XVII, by E. Pichery, Cerf (SC), Paris, 1958.

Early Christian Writings, Penguin, 1987.

John Moscus, *Le pré spirituel*, by Rouet de Journel, Paris, 1946.

Palladius, *Histoire lausiaque*. Introduced by L. Leloir and translated by the Carmelite Sisters of Mazille, DDB, Paris, 1981.

Abbot Isaïe, *Recueil ascétique*. Introduction by Lucien Regnault, translated by H. de Broc, Bellefontaine Abbey (Spiritualité orientale, 7 bis), 1970.

Les Apophtegmes des Pères du désert. Alphabetical series. Translated by J.-Cl. Guy, Bellefontaine Abbey (Spiritualité orientale, 1), 1966.

Les sentences des Pères du désert. New anthology (II), by
L. Regnault and the monks of Solesmes, Solesmes
Abbey, 1970.

Les sentences des Pères du désert. Third anthology (III),
by L. Regnault and the monks of Solesmes, Solesmes
Abbey, 1976.

Les sentences des Pères du désert. Series of the anony-
mous ones, by L. Regnault, Bellefontaine Abbey and
Solesmes Abbey, 1985.

Waddell E., *Desert Fathers*, Constable, 1987.

Ward Benedicta (ed.), *Lives of the Desert Fathers*,
Mowbray, Oxford, 1981.

Ward Benedicta (ed.), *Desert Fathers, Daily readings
with the "Desert of the Heart"*, DLT, 1988.

Ward Benedicta (ed.), *Saying of Desert Fathers,* Mowbray,
Oxford, 1981.